Publishers Note

Unfortunately over the past 300 years some words on several lines of the following play have been lost. These are indicated by [.....] where that occasionally happens.

To the Right Honourable The Earl of Jersey, Lord Chamberlain of His Majesty's Houshold, &c.

My Lord,

If any thing may attone for the Liberty I take in offering this trifle to your Lordship, it is, that I will Engage not to be guilty of the Common Vice of Dedications, nor pretend to give the World an account of the many good qualities they ought to admire in your Lordship. I hope I may reckon on it as some little piece of merit, in an age where there are so many people write Panegyricks, and so few deserve 'em. I am sure you ought not to sit for your Picture, to so ill a hand as mine. Men of your Lordship's Figure and Station, tho Useful and Ornamantal to the Age they live in, are yet reserv'd for the Labours of the Historian, and the Entertainment of Posterity; nor ought to be aspers'd with such pieces of Flattery while living, as may render the true History suspected to those that come after. That which should take up all my Care at present, is most humbly to beg your Lordships pardon for Importuning you upon this account; for imagining that your Lordship, (whose hours are all dedicated to the best and most important uses) can have any leisure for this piece of Poetry. I beg, my Lord, that you will receive it, as it was meant, a mark of my Entire Respect and Veneration.

I hope it may be some advantage to me, that the Town has not receiv'd this Play ill; to have depended meerly upon your Lordships good nature, and have offer'd something without any degree of merit, would have been an unpardonable fault, especially to so good a Judge. The Play it self, as I present it to your Lordship, is a much more perfect Poem than it is in the representation on the Stage. I was led into an Error in the writing of it, by thinking that it would be easier to retrench than to add: But when I was at last necessitated, by reason of the extreme length, to cut off near six hundred Lines, I found that it was maim'd by it to a great disadvantage. The Fable (which has no manner of relation to any part of true History,) was left dark and intricate, for want of a great part of the narration, which was left out in the first Scene; and the Chain and Connexion, which ought to be in the Dialogue, was interrupted in many other places. But since what was omitted in the Acting, is now kept in, I hope it may indifferently Entertain your Lordship at an unbending hour. The faults which are most generally found, (and which I could be very proud of submitting to your Lordship's Judgment, if you can have leisure for so trivial a cause,) are, that the Catastrophe in the fifth Act is barbarous, and shocks the Audience. Some people, whose Judgment I ought to have a deference for, have told me that they wisht I had given the latter part of the story quite another turn; that Artaxerxes and Amestris ought to have been preserv'd, and made happy in the Conclusion of the Play; that besides the satisfaction which the Spectators would have had to have seen two Vertuous (or at least Innocent) Characters, rewarded and successful, there might have been also a more Noble and Instructive Moral drawn that way. I must confess if this be an Error, (as I perhaps it may,) it is a voluntary one and an Error of my Judgment: Since in the writing I actually made such a sort of an Objection to my self; and chose to wind up the story this way. Tragedies have been allow'd, I know, to be written both ways very beautifully. But since Terror and Pity are laid down for the Ends of Tragedy, by the great Master and Father of Criticism, I was always inclin'd to fancy, that the last and remaining Impressions, which ought to be left on the minds of an Audience, should proceed from one of these two. They should be struck with Terror in several parts of the Play, but always Conclude and go away with Pity, a sort of regret proceeding from good nature, which, tho an uneasiness, is not always disagreeable, to the person who feels it. It was this passion that the famous Mr Otway succeeded so well in touching, and must and will at all times affect people, who have any tenderness or humanity. If therefore I had sav'd Artaxerxes and Amestris, I believe (with submission to my Judges) I had destroy'd the greatest occasion for Compassion in the whole Play. Any body may perceive, that she is rais'd to some degrees of happiness, by hearing that her Father and Husband are living, (whom she had suppos'd dead,) and by seeing the Enemy and Persecuter of her Family dying at her feet, purposely, that the turn of her death may be more surprizing and pitiful. As for that part of the Objection, which says, that Innocent persons ought not to be shewn unfortunate; The success and general approbation, which many of the best Tragedies that have been writ, and which were built on that foundation, have met with, will be sufficient answer for me.

That which they call the Poetical Justice, is, I think, strictly observ'd, the two principal Contrivers of Evil, the Statesman and Priest, are punish'd with death; and the Queen is depos'd from her authority by her own Son; which, I suppose, will be allowed as the severest mortification that could happen to a woman of her Imperious temper.

If there can be any excuse for my Entertaining your Lordship with this Detail of Criticisms, it is, That I would have this first mark of the honour I have for your Lordship appear with as few faults as possible. Did not the prevailing Character of your Lordship's Excellent humanity and good nature encourage me, what ought I not to fear from the niceness of your Taste and Judgment? The delicacy of your me reflexions may be very satal to so rough a Draught as this is; but if I will believe, (as I am sure I ought to do) all men that I have heard speak of your Lordship, they bid me hope every thing from your Goodness. This is that I must sincerely own, which made me extremely Ambitious of your Lordship's Patronage for this Piece. I am but too sensible, that there are a multitude of faults in it; but since the good nature of the Town has cover'd, or not taken notice of 'em, I must have so much discretion, as not to look with an affected nicety into 'em my self. With all the Faults and Imperfections which it may have, I must own, I shall be yet very well satisfied with it, if it gives me an opportunity of reckoning my self from this time,

Your Lordship's most Obedient, and devoted humble Servant, N. Rowe.

DRAMATIS PERSONAE
MEN
Artaxerxes, Prince of Persia, Eldest Son to the King Arsaces, by a former Queen.
Artaban, Son to Arsaces, by Artemisa.

The Ambitious Step-Mother by Nicholas Rowe

A TRAGEDY

As 'twas Acted at the New Theatre in Little-Lincolns-Inn-Fields. By His Majesty's Servants.

Nicholas Rowe was born in Little Barford, Bedfordshire, England, on June 20th, 1674.

He was educated at Highgate School, and then at Westminster School under the tutelage of Dr. Busby.

In 1688, Rowe became a King's Scholar, and then in 1691 gained entrance into Middle Temple. This was his father's decision (he was a barrister) who felt that his son had made sufficient progress to study law. While at Middle Temple, he decided that studying law was easier if seen as a system of rational government and impartial justice and not as a series of precedents, or collection of positive precepts.

On his father's death, when he was nineteen, he became the master of a large estate and an independent fortune. His future path now was to ignore law and write poetry with a view to eventually writing plays.

The Ambitious Stepmother, Rowe's first play, produced in 1700 at Lincoln's Inn Fields by Thomas Betterton and set in Persepolis, was well received.

This was followed in 1701 by Tamerlane. In this play the conqueror Timur represented William III, and Louis XIV is denounced as Bajazet. It was for many years regularly acted on the anniversary of William's landing at Torbay.

The Fair Penitent (1703), an adaptation of Massinger and Field's The Fatal Dowry, was pronounced by Dr Johnson as one of the most pleasing tragedies ever written in English. He noted that, "The story is domestic, and therefore easily received by the imagination, and assimilated to common life; the diction is exquisitely harmonious, and soft or spritely as occasion requires."

In 1704, he tried his hand at comedy, with The Biter at Lincoln's Inn Fields. The play is said to have amused no one except the author, and Rowe returned to tragedy in Ulysses (1706). For Johnson, this play was to share the fate of many such plays based on mythological heroes, as, "We have been too early acquainted with the poetical heroes to expect any pleasure from their revival"

The Royal Convert (1707) dealt with the persecutions endured by Aribert, son of Hengist and the Christian maiden Ethelinda. The story was set in England in an obscure and barbarous age. Rodogune was a tragic character, of high spirit and violent passions, yet with a wicked with a soul that would have been heroic if it had been virtuous.

Rowe is however well known for his work on Shakespeare's plays. He published the first 18th century edition of Shakespeare in six volumes in 1709. His practical knowledge of the stage helped him divide the plays into scenes and acts, with entrances and exits of the players noted. The spelling of names was normalized and each play prefixed with a dramatis personae. This 1709 edition was also the first to be illustrated, a frontispiece engraving being provided for each play. Unfortunately, Rowe based his text on the discredited Fourth Folio, a failing which many succeeding him also followed.

Rowe also wrote a short biography of William Shakespeare, entitled, Some Account of the Life of Mr. William Shakespear.

For two years (1709-11) he acted as under-secretary to the Duke of Queensberry when he was principal secretary of state for Scotland.

In Dublin in 1712 a revival of his earlier play, Tamerlane, at a time when political passions were running high, the performance provoked a serious riot.

The Tragedy of Jane Shore, played at Drury Lane with Mrs Oldfield in the title role in 1714. It ran for nineteen nights, and kept the stage longer than any other of Rowe's works. In the play, which consists chiefly of domestic scenes and private distress, the wife is forgiven because she repents, and the husband is honoured because he forgives.

The Tragedy of Lady Jane Grey followed in 1715, and as this play was not successful, it was his last foray into the medium.

Whilst his plays met with little success at the time his poems were received extremely well. Although he was not prolific nor his output large the quality was high.

With the accession to the throne of George I he was made a surveyor of customs, and then, in 1715, he succeeded Nahum Tate as poet laureate. It was the high point of his artistic life.

He was also appointed clerk of the council to the Prince of Wales, and in 1718 was nominated by Lord Chancellor Parker as clerk of the presentations in Chancery.

Nicholas Rowe died on December 6th, 1718, and was buried in Westminster Abbey.

Rowe married first a daughter of a Mr Parsons and left a son John. By his second wife Anne, née Devenish, he had a daughter Charlotte.

Index of Contents

Memnon, Formerly General to Arsaces, now disgrac'd; a friend to Artaxerxes.
Mirza, First Minister of State, in the interest of Artemisa and Artaban.
Magas, Priest of the Sun, friend to Mirza and the Queen.
Cleanthes, Friend to Artaban.
Orchanes, Captain of the Guards to the Queen.
WOMEN
Artemisa, Formerly the Wife of Tiribasus a Persian Lord, now married to the King, and Queen of Persia.
Amestris, Daughter to Memnon, in love with, and belov'd by Artaxerxes.
Cleone, Daughter to Mirza, in love with Artaxerxes, and belov'd by Artaban.
Beliza, Confident to Cleone.

THE PROLOGUE

Spoke by **MR BATTERTON**

If Dying Lovers yet deserve a Tear,
If a sad story of a Maids despair,
Yet move Compassion in the pitying fair,
This day the Poet does his Art employ,
The soft accesses of your Souls to try.
Nor let the Stoick boast his mind unmov'd,
The Brute Philosopher, who ne're has prov'd
The Joy of Loving or of being Lov'd;
Who scorns his humane nature to confess,
And striving to be more than man, is less.
Nor let the men, the weeping fair accuse
Those kind protectors of the Tragick Muse,
Whose Tears did moving Otway's labours crown,
And made the poor Monimia's Grief their own:
Those Tears, their art, not weakness has confest,
Their Grief approv'd the niceness of their taste,
And they wept most, because they judg'd the best.
O cou'd this Age's Writers hope to find
An Audience to Compassion thus inclin'd,
The Stage would need no Farce, nor Song nor Dance,
Nor Capering Monsieur brought from Active France.
Clinch and his Organ Pipe, his Dogs and Bear,
To native Barnet might again repair,
Or breathe with Captain Otter, Bankside Air.
Majestick Tragedy shou'd once agen
In Purple Pomp adorn the swelling Scene.
Her search shou'd ransack all the Ancient's store,
The Fortunes of their Loves and Arms explore,
Such as might grieve you, but shou'd please you more.
What Shakespear durst not, this bold Age shou'd do,
And famous Greek and Latian Beauties show.

Shakespear, whose Genius to its self a Law,
Cou'd men in every height of Nature draw,
And Copy'd all but women that he saw.
Those Ancient Heroines your concern shou'd move,
Their Grief and Anger much, but most their Love;
For in the account of every Age we find
The best and fairest of that Sex were kind,
To Pity always, and to Love inclin'd.
Assert, ye fair ones, who in Judgment sit,
Your Ancient Empire over Love and Wit;
Reform our Sense, and teach the men t' Obey,
They'll leave their Tumbling if you lead the way.
Be but what those before to Otway were;
O were you but as kind, we know you are as fair.

ACT I

SCENE I. A Royal Palace

Enter at several Doors **MIRZA** and **MAGAS**.

MIRZA
What bringst thou, Magas? Say, how fares the King?

MAGAS
As one, whom when we number with the living,
We say the most we can; tho sure it must
Be happier far, to quit a wretched being,
Than keep it on such terms: For as I enter'd
The Royal Lodging, an universal horror
Struck thro my Eyes, and chill'd my very Heart;
The chearful day was every where shut out
With care, and left a more than midnight darkness,
Such as might ev'n be felt: A few dim Lamps,
That feebly lifted up their sickly heads,
Lookt faintly thro the shade, and made it seem
More dismal by such light; while those that waited,
In solemn sorrow, mixt with wild amazement,
Observ'd a dreadful silence.

MIRZA
Didst thou see him?

MAGAS
My Lord, I did; treading with gentle steps,
I reacht the Bed, which held the poor remains

Of great Arsaces, just as I approacht,
His drooping lids, that seem'd for ever clos'd,
Were faintly rear'd, to tell me that he liv'd:
The balls of sight, dim and depriv'd of motion,
Sparkled no more with that Majestick sire,
At which ev'n Kings have trembled; but had lost
Their common useful office, and were shaded
With an eternal night; struck with a sight,
That shew'd me humane nature faln so low,
I hastily retir d.

MIRZA
He dyes too soon;
And fate if possible must be delay d;
The thought that labours in my forming brain,
Yet crude and immature, demands more time.
Have the Physicians giv'n up all their hopes?
Cannot they add a few days to a Monarch,
In recompence of thousand vulgar fates,
Which their Drugs daily hasten?

MAGAS
As I past
The outward Rooms, I found 'em in Consult;
I askt 'em if their art was at a stand,
And could not help the King; they shook their heads,
And in most grave and solemn wise, unfolded
Matter, which little purported, but words
Rankt in right learned phrase; all I could learn, was;
That Nature's kindly warmth was quite extinct,
Nor could the breath of art kindle again
Th' Etherial fire.

MIRZA
My Royal Mistress Artemisa's fate,
And all her Son Young Artaban's high hopes,
Hang on this lucky Crisis; since this day.
The haughty Artaxerxes and old Memnon

[Enter **PERSEPOLIS**.

The yearly Feast
Devoted to our glorious God the Sun,
Hides their designs under a holy veil;
And thus Religion is a mask for Faction.
But let their Guardian Genii still be watchful,
For if they chance to nod, my waking vengeance
Shall surely catch that moment to destroy 'em.

MAGAS
'Tis said the fair Amestris, Memnon's Daughter,
Comes in their company.

MIRZA
That fatal Beauty,
With most malignant influence, has crost
My first and great Ambition. When my Brother,
The great Cleander fell by Memnon's hand,
(You know the story of our Houses quarrel)
I sought the King for Justice on the Murderer;
And to confirm my interest in the Court,
In confidence of mighty wealth and power,
A long descent from Noble Ancestors,
And somewhat of the Beauty of the Maid,
I offer'd my Cleone to the Prince
Fierce Artaxerxes; he, with rude disdain
Refus'd the proffer; and to grate me more,
Publickly own'd his passion for Amestris;
And in despight ev'n of his Fathers Justice,
Espous'd the Cause of Memnon.

MAGAS
Ev'n from that noted Aera, I remember
You dated all your service to the Queen,
Our Common Mistress.

MIRZA
'Tis true, I did so; Nor was it in vain;
She did me right, and satisfy'd my vengeance;
Memnon was banisht, and the Prince disgrac'd
Went into Exile with him. Since that time,
Since I have been admitted to her Council,
And have seen her, with unerring judgment guide
The Reins of Empire, I have been amaz'd,
To see her more than manly strength of Soul,
Cautious in good success, in bad unshaken;
Still arm'd against the uncertain turns of Chance,
Untoucht by any weakness of her Sex,
Their Superstition, Pity, or their Fear;
And is a Woman only in her Cunning.
What story tells of great Semiramis,
Or Rolling Time, that gathers as it goes,
Has added more, such Artemisa is.

MAGAS
Sure 'twas a mark of an uncommon Genius,

To bend a Soul like that of great Arsaces,
And Charm him to her sway.

MIRZA
Certainly Fate,
Or somewhat like the force of Fate, was in it;
And still whene're remembrance sets that scene
Before my eyes, I view it with amazement.

MAGAS
I then was young, a stranger to the Court,
And only took the story as reported
By different Fame, you must have known it better.

MIRZA
Indeed I did, then favour'd by the King,
And by that means a sharer in the secret.
'Twas on a day of publick Festival,
When Beauteous Artemisa stood to view,
Behind the Covert of a Golden Lattice,
When King and Court returning from the Temple;
When just as by her stand Arsaces past,
The Windows, by design or chance, fell down,
And to his view expos'd her blushing Beauties.
She seem'd surpriz'd, and presently withdrew,
But ev'n that moment was an age in Love;
So was the Monarchs heart for passion moulded,
So apt to take at first the soft impression.
Soon as we were alone, I found the Evil
Already past a Remedy, and vainly
Urg'd the resentment of her injur'd Lord:
His Love was deaf to all.

MAGAS
Was Tiribasus absent?

MIRZA
He was then General of the Horse,
Under old Memnon in the Median War.
But if that distant view so much had charm'd him,
Imagine how he burnt, when, by my means,
He view'd her Beauties nearer, when each action,
And every graceful sound conspir'd to charm him:
Joy of her Conquest, and the hopes of Greatness,
Gave Lustre to her Charms, and made her seem
Of more than mortal Excellence. In short,
After some faint resistance, like a Bride
That strives a while, tho eager for the bliss,

The furious King Enjoy'd her.
And to secure their Joys, a snare was laid
For her unthinking Lord, in which he fell
Before the fame of this could reach his Ears.
Since that, she still has by successful Arts
Maintain'd that power, which first her beauty gain'd.

MAGAS
With deepest foresight, wisely has she laid
A sure foundation of the future greatness
Of Artaban, her only darling Son.
Each busie thought, that rouls within her breast,
Labours for him; the King, when first he sicken'd,
Declar'd he should succeed him in the Throne.

MIRZA
That was a point well gain'd; nor were the Eldership
Of Artaxerxes worth our least of fears,
If Memnon's interest did not prop his Cause.
Since then they stand secur'd, by being joyn'd,
From reach of open force; it were a Masterpiece
Worthy a thinking head, to sow division
And seeds of jealousie, to lose those bonds,
Which knit and hold 'em up, that so divided,
With ease they might be ruin'd.

MAGAS
That's a difficulty, next to impossible.

MIRZA
Cease to think so;
The wise and active conquer difficulties,
By daring to attempt 'em; sloth and folly
Shiver and shrink at sight of toil and hazard,
And make th' impossibility they fear;
Ev'n Memnon's temper seems to give th' occasion;
Of wrong impatient, headlong to revenge;
Tho bold, yet wants that faculty of thinking,
That should direct his anger. Valiant fools
Were made by Nature for the wise to work with;
They are their tools, and 'tis the sport of Statesmen,
When Heroes knock their knotty heads together,
And fall by one another.

MAGAS
What you've said,
Has wak'd a thought in me which may be lucky;
Ere he was banisht for your Brothers murder,

There was a friendship 'twixt us; and tho then
I left his barren soil, to root my self
More safely, under your auspicious shade,
Yet still pretending tyes of ancient Love,
At his arrival here I'll visit him;
Whence this advantage may at least be made,
To ford his shallow Soul.

MIRZA

Oh much, much more;
'Twas happily remembred, nothing gulls
These open, unsuspecting fools, like friendship;
Dull heavy things! whom Nature has left honest
In meer frugality, to save the Charge
She's at in setting out a thinking Soul:
Who, since their own short understandings reach
No farther than the present, think ev'n the wise,
Like them, disclose the secrets of their breasts,
Speak what they think, and tell tales of themselves:
Thy function too will varnish o're our arts,
And sanctifie dissembling.

MAGAS

Yet still I doubt,
His caution may draw back, and fear a snare.

MIRZA

Tell him, the better to assist the fraud,
That ev'n I wish his friendship, and would gladly
Forget that cause of hate, which long has held us
At mortal distance, give up my revenge,
A grateful Offering to the publick peace.

MAGAS

Could you afford him such a bribe as that,
A Brothers blood yet unatton'd—

MIRZA

No Magas,
It is not in the power of fate to raze
That thought from out my memory;
Eternal night, 'tis true, may cast a shade
On all my faculties, extinguish knowledge;
And great Revenge may with my Being cease;
But while I am, that ever will remain,
And in my latest Spirits still survive.
Yet, I would have thee promise that, and more,
The friendship of the Queen, the restitution

Of his Command, and Honours, that his Daughter
Shall be the Bride of Artaban; say any thing;
Thou knowst the Faith of Courtiers, and their Oaths,
Like those of Lovers, the Gods laugh at 'em.

MAGAS
Doubt not my zeal to serve our Royal Mistress,
And in her Interest yours, my Friend and Patron.

MIRZA
My worthy Priest! still be my friend, and share
The utmost of my power, by greatness rais'd.

[Embracing.

Thou like the God thou serv'st, shall shine aloft,
And with thy influence rule the under world.
But see! the Queen appears; she seems to muse,
Her thoughtful Soul, labours with some event
Of high import, which bustles like an Embryo
In its dark room, and longs to be disclos'd.
Retire, lest we disturb her.
They retire to the side of the Stage.

[Enter the **QUEEN** attended.

QUEEN
Be fixt, my Soul, fixt on thy own firm basis!
Be constant to thy self; nor know the weakness,
The poor Irresolution of my Sex:
Disdain those shews of danger, that would bar
My way to glory. Ye Diviner Pow'rs!
By whom 'tis said we are, from whose bright Beings
Those active sparks were struck which move our clay,
I feel, and I Confess the Etherial energy,
That busie restless principle, whose appetite
Is only pleas'd with greatness like your own:
Why have you clogg'd it then with dull mass,
And shut it up in Woman? Why debas'd it
To an Inferiour part of the Creation?
Since, your own heavenly hands mistook my lot,
'Tis you have err'd, not I. Could Fate e're mean
Me, for a Wife, a Slave to Tiribasus!
To such a thing as he! a Wretch! a Husband!
Therefore in just assertion of my self,
I shook him off, and past those narrow limits,
Which Laws contrive in vain for Souls born great.
There is not, must not be a bound for greatness;

Power gives a sanction, and makes all things just.
Ha! Mirza! Worthy Lord! I saw thee not,

[Seeing **MIRZA**.

So busie were my faculties in thought.

MIRZA
The thoughts of Princes dwell in sacred privacy,
Unknown and venerable to the vulgar;

[Bowing.

And like a Temples innermost recesses,
None enters, to behold the hallow'd mysteries,
Unbidden of the God that dwells within.

QUEEN
Wise Mirza! were my Soul a Temple, fit
For Gods, and Godlike Counsels to inhabit,
Thee only would I choose of all mankind,
To be the Priest, still favour'd with access;
Whose piercing Wit, sway'd by unerring Judgment,
Might mingle ev'n with assembled Gods,
When they devise unchangeable decrees,
And call 'em Fate.

MIRZA
Whate're I am, each faculty,
The utmost power of my Exerted Soul,
Preserves a being only for your service;
And when I am not yours, I am no more:

QUEEN
Time shall not know an end of my acknowledgments,
But every day of our continu'd lives
Be witness of my gratitude, to draw
The knot, which holds our Common Interest, closer;
Within six days, my Son, my Artaban,
Equally dear to me as life and glory,
In publick shall Espouse the fair Cleone,
And be my pledge of Everlasting Amity.

MIRZA
O Royal Lady! you out-bid my service;
And all returns are vile, but words the poorest.

QUEEN

Enough! be as thou hast been, still my friend,
I ask no more. But I observe of late,
Your Daughter grows a stranger to the Court;
Know you the cause?

MIRZA
A melancholy Girl;
Such in her Infancy her Temper was,
Soft ev'n beyond her Sexes tenderness;
By nature pitiful, and apt to grieve
For the mishaps of others, and so make
The sorrows of the wretched world her own.
Her Closet and the Gods share all her time,
Except when (only by some Maid attended)
She seeks some shady solitary Grove,
Or by the gentle murmur of some Brook
Sits sadly listning to a tale of sorrow,
Till with her tears she swell the narrow stream.

QUEEN
It is not well, these thoughts must be remov'd:
That eating Canker Grief, with wasteful spight,
Preys on the Rosie bloom of Youth and Beauty:
But Love shall chace away these clouds of sadness;
My Son shall breathe so warm a gale of sighs,
As shall dissolve those Isicles, that hang
Like death about her heart.
Attend us, holy Magus, to the King,
Nor cease to importune the mighty Gods
To grant him health, tho much I fear in vain.

[Exit **QUEEN**, **MAGAS**, and **ATTENDANTS**.

[Manet **MIRZA**.

MIRZA
This meddling Priest longs to be found a fool;
Thinks he that Memnon, Souldier as he is,
Thoughtless, and dull, will listen to his soothing?
Howe're, I gave his wise proposal way,
Nay, urg'd him to go on; the shallow fraud
Will ruine him for ever with my Enemies,
And make him firmly mine, spight of his fears
And natural inconstancy.
While Choice remains he will be still unsteady,
And nothing but necessity can fix him.

[Exit.

[Enter **ARTAXERES**, **MEMNON** and **ATTENDANTS**.

ARTAXERES
Methinks, my noble Father and my Friend,
We enter here like strangers, and unlookt for:
Each busie face we meet, with wonder starts,
And seems amaz'd to see us.

MEMNON
Well may th' ignoble herd
Start, if with heedless steps they unawares
Tread on the Lyons walk; a Prince's genius
Awes with supiner greatness all beneath him.
With wonder they behold the great Arsaces
Reviv'd again in Godlike Artaxerxes.
In you they see him, such as oft they did
Returning from his Wars, and Crown'd with Conquest,
When all our Virgins met him on the way,
And with their Songs and Dances blest his Triumph:
Now basely aw'd by factious Priests and Women,
They start at Majesty, and seem surpriz'd
As if a God had met 'em. In Honours name
Why have we let this be? Why have we languisht?
And suffer'd such a Government as this
To waste our strength, and wear our Empire low?

ARTAXERES
Curst be the means by which these ills arose,
Fatal alike to me as to my Country;
Which my great Soul, unable to revenge,
Has yet with indignation only seen,
Cut off by Arts of Coward Priests and Statesmen,
Whom I disdain'd with servile smiles to court,
From the great right which God and Nature gave,
My birthright to a Throne.

MEMNON
Nor Priests, nor Statesmen,
Could have compleated such an ill as that,
If Woman had not mingled in the mischief;
If Artimesa had not, by her Charms,
And all her Sex's Cunning, wrought the King,
Old, obvious to her arts, decay'd in greatness,
Dead to the memory of what once he was,
Just crawling on the verge of wretched life,
A burthen to himself, and his friends pity;
Among his other failings, to forget

All that a Father and a King could owe
To such a Son as you were; to cut you off
From your Succession, from your hopes of Empire,
And graft her upstart offspring on to Royalty.

ARTAXERES
But if I beat it,
Oh may I live to be my Brothers Slave,
The scorn of those brave Friends that own my Cause;
May you my Father spurn me for a Coward,
May all my noble hopes of Love and Glory
Leave me to vile despair. By heaven, my heart
Sits lighter in my bosome, when I think
That I this day shall meet the Boy my Brother,
Whose young Ambition with aspiring wings
Dares ev'n to mate my greatness.

MEMNON
Fame, that speaks
Minutely every circumstance of Princes,
Describes him bold, and fiercely fond of power,
Which ev'n in spight of Nature he affects.
Impatient of Command, and hardly daigning
To be controll'd by his Imperious Mother.
'Tis said too (as no means were left untry'd,
Which might prepare and fit him to contend
With a superiour right of birth and merit,)
That Books, and the politer Arts, (which those
Who know admire) have been his care; already
He mingles in their Councils, and they trust
His youth with secrets of important villany.
The Crowd, taught by his Creatures to admire him,
Stile him a God in Wisdom.

ARTAXERES
Be that his glory,
Let him with Pedants hunt for praise in Books,
Pore out his Life amongst the lazy Gown-men,
Grow old and vainly proud in fancy'd knowledge,
Unequal to the task of vast Ambition.
Ambition! the desire of active Souls,
That pushes 'em beyond the bounds of Nature,
And elevates the Hero to the Gods.
But see! my Love, your beauteous Daughter comes,
And ev'n Ambition ckens at her sight.

[Enter **AMESTRIS** attended.

Revenge, and fierce desires of Glory, cease
To urge my passions, master'd by her eyes;
And only gentle fires now warm my breast.

AMESTRIS [To **MEMNON**]
I come, my Father, to attend your order.

MEMNON
'Tis well; and I would have thee still be near me,
The malice of the Faction which I hate,
Would vent it self even on thy Innocence,
Wert thou not safe under a Fathers Care.

ARTAXERES
Oh say a Lover's too; nor can you have
An Interest in her safety more than mine.
Love gives a Right superiour ev'n to Nature;
Or Love is Nature, in the noblest meaning,
The cause and the preserver of the world.
These arms that long to press thee to my bosome,
For ever shall defend thee.

MEMNON
Therefore, my Son,
Unto your Care I leave our common charge;
Tigranes with our friends expects my orders;
Those when I have dispatcht, upon the instant
I will return, and meet at your apartment.

[Exit **MEMNON**.

ARTAXERES
Come to my arms, and let me hide thee there
From all those fears that vex thy beating heart,
Be safe and free from all those fancy'd dangers,
That haunt thy Apprehension.

AMESTRIS
Can you blame me?
If from retirement drawn and pleasing solitude,
I fear to tempt this Stormy Sea the World,
Whose every Beach is strew'd with wrecks of wretches,
That daily perish in it. Curst Ambition!
Why dost thou come to trouble my repose,
Who have even from my Infancy disclaim'd thee?

ARTAXERES
Cease to complain, my Love, and let no thought

But what brings peace and joy approach thy breast.
Let me impart my manly fires to thee,
To warm thy fancy to a taste of-glory;
Imperial power and Purple greatness wait thee,
And sue for thy acceptance; by the Sun,
And by Arsaces Head, I will not mount
The Throne of Cyrus, but to share it with thee.

AMESTRIS
Vain shews of happiness! deceitful pageantry!
Ah! Prince, hadst thou but known the joys which dwell
With humbler fortunes, thou wouldst Curse thy Royalty.
Had fate alotted us some obscure Village,
Where only blest with life's necessities,
We might have pass'd in peace our happy days,
Free from the Cares which Crowns and Empires bring;
There no Step-mother, no Ambitious Brother,
No wicked Statesmen, would with Impious Arts,
Have strove to wrest from us our small Inheritance,
Or stir the simple Hinds to noisie faction.
Our nights had all been blest with balmy slumbers,
And all our waking hours been crown'd with Love.

ARTAXERES
Exquisite Charmer! now by Orosmades
I swear, thy each soft accent melts my Soul:
The joy of Conquest, and Immortal Triumph,
Honour and Greatness, all that fires the Hero
To high Exploits, and Everlasting Fame,
Grows vile in sight of thee. My haughty Soul,
By Nature fierce, and panting after glory,
Could be content to live obscure with thee,
Forgotten and unknown of all but my Amestris.

AMESTRIS
No, Son of great Arsaces, though my Soul
Shares in my Sexes weakness, and would fly
From noise and faction, and from fatal greatness,
Yet for thy sake, thou Idol of my heart,
(Nor will I blush to own the sacred flame,
Thy sighs and vows have kindled in my breast,)
For thy lov'd sake, spight of my boding fears,
I'll meet the danger which Ambition brings,
And tread one path with thee: Nor shalt thou lose
The glorious portion which thy fate designs thee,
For thy Amestris fears.

ARTAXERES

Give me those fears;
For all things will be well.

AMESTRIS
Grant it, ye powers:
This day before your Altars will I kneel,
Where all my Vows shall for my Prince be offer'd:
Still let success attend him, Let mankind
Adore in him your visible divinity;
Nor will I importune you for my self,
But summ up all I ask in Artaxerxes.

ARTAXERES
And doubt not but the Gods will kindly hear
Their Virgin Votary, and grant her Pray'r;
Our glorious Sun, the source of light and heat,
Whose influence chears the world he did create,
Shall smile on thee from his Meridian Skies,
And own the kindred Beauties of thy Eyes;
Thy Eyes, which, could his own fair beams decay,
Might shine for him, and bless the world with day.

[Exeunt.

ACT II

SCENE I. An Apartment in the Palace

Enter **MEMNON** and **MAGAS**.

MEMNON
Those who are wise in Courts, my holy Sir,
Make friendships with the Ministers of State,
Nor seek the ruines of a wretched Exile,
Lest there should be Contagion in misfortunes,
And make the alliance fatal.

MAGAS
Friends like Memnon
Are worth being sought in danger; since this age
Of most flagitious note, degenerates
From the fam'd vertue of our Ancestors,
And leaves but few Examples of their Excellence.
Whom should we seek for friendships but those few,
Those happy few, within whose breasts alone,
The footsteps of lost vertue yet remain?

MEMNON

I prithee peace! for nothing misbecomes
The man that would be thought a friend, like flattery;
Flattery! the meanest kind of base dissembling,
And only us'd to catch the grossest fools:
Besides, it stains the honour of thy function,
Which like the Gods thou servst, should be sincere.

MAGAS

By that sincerity, by all the service
My friendship can express, I would approve it;
And tho I went not from Persepolis
Companion of your exile, yet my Heart
Was with you still; and what I could I did,
Beseeching every God for your return;
Nor were those Vows in vain, since once again
'Tis given me to behold my friend, nay more,
Would you agree, to keep you here for ever.

MEMNON

The Gods, 'tis true, are just, and have, I hope,
At length decreed an end of my misfortunes;
At least they give me this, to dye with honour,
When Life grows vile or burthensome.

MAGAS

By me they offer all that you can ask,
And point an easie way to happiness.
Spare then the Wounds our wretched Country fears,
The thousand ills which Civil discord brings,
Oh still that noise of war, whose dread alarms,
Frightens repose from Country Villages,
And stirs rude tumult up and wild distraction,
In all our peaceful Cities.

MEMNON

Witness for me,
Ye awful Gods, who view our inmost thoughts!
I took not arms, till urg'd by self defence,
The eldest law of Nature.
Impute not then those ills which may insue
To me, but those who with incessant hate
Pursue my life; whose malice spreads the flame
To every part, that my devoted fabrick
May in the universal ruine burn.

MAGAS

And yet ev'n there perhaps you judge too rashly;
Impetuous passion hurries you so fast,
You cannot mark the advantage of your fortune.

MEMNON
Has not the Law been urg'd to set a brand
Of foul dishonour on my hoary head?
Ha! am I not proscrib'd?

MAGAS
Forget that thought,
That jarring grates your Soul, and turns the harmony
Of blessed peace to curst infernal discord.
Hate and its fatal causes all shall cease,
And Memnon's name be honour'd as of old,
The bravest and the most successful warrior,
The fortunate defender of his Country.

MEMNON
'Tis true, (nor will it seem a boast to own)
I have fought well for Persia, and repay'd
The benefit of birth with honest service,
Full fifty years harnest in rugged Steel,
I have endur'd the biting Winters blast,
And the severer heats of parching Summer;
While they who loll'd at home on lazy Couches,
Amidst a Crew of Harlots and soft Eunuchs,
Were at my cost secure in luxury,
This is a Justice Mirza's self must do me.

MAGAS
Even he, tho fatal accidents have set
A most unhappy bar between your friendship,
Lamenting that there had been cause of Enmity,
And owning all the merit of your virtues,
Will often wish Fate had ordain d you friends.

MEMNON
Our God the Sun shall sooner change his Course,
And all the impossibilities, which Poets
Count to extravagance of loose discription,
Shall sooner be.

MAGAS
Yet hear me, noble Memnon;
When by the duty of my Priesthood mov'd,
And in just detestation of the mischiefs
Intestine jars produce, I urg'd wise Mirza,

By his Concurrence, Help, and healing Counsels,
To stop those wounds at which his Country bleeds;
Griev'd at the thought, he vow d, his whole endeavour
Should be to close those breaches:
That even Cleander's death, and all those Quarrels
That long have nourisht hatred in your Houses,
Should be in joy of publick Peace forgotten.

MEMNON
Oh couldst thou charm the malice of a Statesman,
And make him quit his purpose of Revenge,
Thy preaching might reform the guilty world,
And Vice would be no more.

MAGAS
Nay, ev'n the Queen
Will bind the Confirmation by her Son,
And asks the fair Amestris for Prince Artaban.

MEMNON
Were that the only terms, it were impossible.

MAGAS
You would not shun th' alliance of a Prince?

MEMNON
No; for it is the glory of my fate,
That Artaxerxes is design'd my Son,
With every Grace and Royal Vertue crown'd;
Great, just and merciful, such as mankind,
(When, in the infant world, first governments
Began by chance) would have design'd a King.

MAGAS
Unbounded power, and height of greatness, give
To Kings that lustre, which we think divine;
The wise who know 'em, know they are but men,
Nay, sometimes weak ones too; the Crowd indeed,
Who kneel before the Image, not the God,
Worship the Deity their hands have made.
The Name of Artaban will be as great
As that of Cyrus, when he shall possess
(As sure he shall) his Throne.

MEMNON
Ha! what means he!
This Villain Priest! but hold my rage a little,
And learn dissimulation; I'll try him farther.

[Aside.
You talk in Riddles, when you name a Throne
And Artaban, the Gods, who portion out
The Lots of Princes as of private men,
Have put a bar between his hopes and Empire.

MAGAS
What bar?

MEMNON
The best, an Elder Brothers Claim.

MAGAS
That's easily remov'd, the King their Father
On just and weighty reasons has decreed
His Scepter to the younger; add to this,
The joint Concurrence of our Persian Lords,
Who only want your voice to make it firm.

MEMNON
Can I? Can they? Can any honest hand,
Join in an act like this? is not the Elder
By nature pointed out for preference?
Is not his right inroll'd amongst those Laws
Which keep the world's vast frame in beauteous order?
Ask those thou namest but now, what made them Lords?
What titles had they had, if merit only
Could have conferr'd a right? if Nature had not
Strove hard to thrust the worst deserving first,
And stampt the Noble mark of Eldership
Upon their baser mettal?

MAGAS
Sure there may be
Reasons, of so much power and cogent force,
As may even set aside this right of Birth,
If Sons have rights, yet Fathers have 'em too.
'Twere an Invidious task to enter into
The Insolence, and other faults, which mov'd
Royal Arsaces, to a just displeasure
Against his Eldest Son Prince Artaxerxes.

MEMNON
Ha! dare not for thy life, I charge dare not
To brand the spotless virtue of my Prince,
With falshoods of most base and damn'd contrivance.
I tell thee, envious Priest, should the just Gods
Require severe account of thy past life,

And charge remembrance to dispose thy Crimes,
In rank and hideous order to thy view,
Horror and guilt of Soul would make thee mad.

MAGAS
You take the matter farther than I meant it;
My friendship only aims at your advantage,
Would point you out a way to Peace and Honour,
And in return of this, your rage unkindly
Loads me with Injuries.

MEMNON
Away! I cannot bear thy base dissembling,
My honest Soul disdains thee and thy friendship.
How hast thou dar'd to think so vilely of me;
That I would condescend to thy mean arts,
And traffick with thee for a Princes ruin;
A Prince! the Joy and Honour of Mankind,
As much superiour to the rest of Kings,
As they themselves are above common men,
And is the very Image of the Gods,
Wer't thou not priviledg'd, like age and women,
My Sword should reach thee, and revenge the wrong
Thy Tongue has done his fame.

MAGAS
Ungrateful Lord!
Would'st thou invade my life, as a return
For proffer'd Love? But let th' event declare
How great a good by me sincerely offer'd,
Thy dull Romantick honour has refus'd.
And since I have discharg'd the debt I ow'd
To former friendship, if the Gods hereafter
Send Ruin down, and plague thee with Confusion,
Remember me in vain, and Curse thy folly.

[Exit **MAGAS**.

MEMNON
No my remembrance treasures honest thoughts,
And holds not things like thee; I scorn thy friendship;
And would not owe my life to such a Villain;
But thou art hardly Saint enough to prophecy.
Were all thy Tribe like thee, it might well startle
Our Lay unlearned faith, when thro such hands
The knowledge of the Gods is reach'd to man.
But thus those Gods instruct us, that not all
(Who like intruders thrust into their service,

And turn the Holy Office to a trade,)
Participate their sacred influence.
This then is your own Cause, ye awful powers,
Revenge your selves, your violated Altars,
That those who with unhallow'd hands approach,
May tremble at your justice.

[Exit **MEMNON**.

SCENE II. The Palace

Enter the **QUEEN**, **ARTABAN**, **MIRZA**, **MAGAS**, and **ATTENDANTS**.

ARTABAN
My Brother then is come.

MIRZA
My Lord, I saw him,
With him old haughty Memnon; as they past,
With fierce disdain they view'd the gazing Crowd,
And with dumb Pride seem'd to neglect that worship
Which yet they wisht to sind; this way they move,
'Tis said to ask an Audience of the King.

QUEEN
Mirza, 'tis well, I thank thy timely care;
Here will we face this storm of insolence,
Nor fear the noisy, thunder, let it rowl,
Then burst, and spend at once its idle rage.

ARTABAN
Why meet we thus like wrangling Advocates,
To urge the justice of our Cause with words?
I hate this parle, 'tis tame; if we must meet,
Give me my Arms, and let us stake at once
Our rights of Merit and of Eldership,
And prove like Men our title.

MIRZA
'Twere unsafe,
They come surrounded by a croud of friends,
To strike thro these were dangerous and rash,
Fate waits for 'em elsewhere with certain ruine;
From Mirza's hand expect it.

QUEEN

Be it so:
Auspicions Sage, I trust thee with my fortune,
My hopes of greatness, do thou guide 'em all,
For me and for thy self. My Son give way,
Nor let thy hasty youth disturb with outrage
The present necessary face of peace;
Occasions great and glorious will remain
Worthy thy Arms and Courage.

ARTABAN
I obey;
And willingly resign th' unmanly task,
Words are indeed your province.

MIRZA
My Royal Mistress,
Prepare to meet with more than brutal fury
From the fierce Prince and Memnon.

QUEEN
Well I know
The Insolence and native Pride of each,
With scurril taunts and blackest infamy
They load my name: But let the wretches rail,
A woman's vengeance waits 'em.

MIRZA
They are here.

[Enter **ARTAXERES**, **MEMNON**, and **ATTENDANTS**.

ARTAXERES
Ye tutelar Gods, who guard this Royal fabrick,
And thou, O Orosmades, the Protector
Of the great Persian race. E're yet my Father,
Royal Arsaces, mingle with your God heads,
Grant me once more to lay before his feet
His eldest-born, his once lov'd Artaxerxes,
To offer my Obedience to his Age;
All that a Son can owe to such a Father.
You, who with haggard eyes stare wildly on me,
If (as by your attendance here you seem)
You serve the King my Father, lead me to him.

QUEEN
And dost thou wonder that mankind should start,
When Parricides and Rebels, in despight
Of Nature, Majesty, and Reverend Age,

With Impious force, and Ruffian violence,
Would rob a King and Father of his life;
Cut off his short remains—

ARTAXERES
Ha! sayst thou, woman;
I prethee peace, and urge not a reply,
I would not hold acquaintance with thy Infamy.

QUEEN
Ye Righteous powers, whose justice awes the world,
Let not your Thunders sleep when Crimes like these
Stalk in the open air.

ARTAXERES
Thy Priest instructs thee,
Else sure thou hadst not dar'd to tempt the Gods,
And trifle with their Justice: Canst thou name it
And look on me? on me, whom thy Curst arts
Have strove to bar from native Right to Empire,
Made me a stranger to a Fathers Love,
And broke the bands of Nature, which once held me
The nea rest to his heart.

QUEEN
Had he not reason,
When thou with Rebel Insolence didst dare
To own and to protect that hoary Ruffian;

[Pointing to **MEMNON**.

And in dispight ev'n of thy Fathers justice,
To stir the factious Rabble up to arms
For him; and make a murderer's cause thy own.

MEMNON
I had another name (nor shouldst thou move me,
Insulting Queen, to words, did not remembrance
With horror sting my Soul for Tiribasus,
Thy murder'd Tiribasus) when by my fatal orders,
And by his own high Courage urg'd, he fell,
To make thy way to guilty greatness easie.
I thought him then a Traytor (for thy arts
Had taught the Royal Mandate so to call him)
Too big for publick Justice, and on that pretence
Consented to the snare, that catcht his life;
So my obedient honesty was made
The Pandar to thy Lust and black Ambition.

Except the guilt of that accursed day,
In all my Iron years of wars and danger,
From blooming youth down to decaying age,
My fame ne're knew a stain of foul dishonour,
And if that make me guilty, think what thou art,
The Cause and the Contriver of that mischief.

QUEEN
What namest thou Tiribasus, be his guilt
Forgotten with his memory. Think on Cleander,
And let the Furies that enquire for blood,
Stir horror up, and bitterest remorse,
To gnaw thy anxiou Soul. Oh great Cleande
Unworthy was thy fate, thou first of Warriors,
To fall beneath a base Assassin's stab,
Whom all the thirsty instruments of death,
Had in the field of Battel sought in vain.

MEMNON
In sight of Heaven, and of the equal Gods,
I will avow that my Revenge was just;
My injur'd honour could not ask for less:
Since he refus'd to do a Souldiers Justice,
I us'd him as I ought.

QUEEN
Amazing boldness!
And dare'st thou call that act a Souldiers Justice?
Didst thou not meet him with dissembled Friendship,
Hiding the rancour of thy heart in smiles;
When he (whose open unsuspecting nature
Thought thee a Souldier honest as himself)
Came to the Banquet, as secure of peace,
By mutual vows renew'd; and in the revel
Of that luxurious day, forgetting hate,
And every cause of ancient animosity,
Devoted all his thoughts to mirth and friendship;
Then Memnon (at an hour when few are Villains
The sprightly juice infusing gentler thoughts,
And kindling love ev'n in the coldest breasts,)
Unequal to him in the face of War,
Stole on Cleander with a Cowards malice,
And struck him to the heart.

MEMNON
By the stern God,
By Mars, the Patron of my honour'd Wars,
'Tis basely false: In his own drunken brawl

The boaster fell. I bore his lavish tongue,
Nor thought him worth my Sword, till (his cold temper
Warm'd with the Wine) he dar'd me to the Combat,
Then pleas'd to meet him in that fit of Valour,
I took him at his word, and (with my Sword
Drawn against his in equal opposition)
I kill'd him, while it lasted.

ARTAXERES
Cease we, my friend,
This womens war of railing, when they talk,
Men should be still, and let noise tire it self.
I came to find a Father, tho my fears
Suggest the worst of evils to my thoughts,
And make me dread to hear Arsaces fate.
Lead, Memnon, to the Presence.

QUEEN
Prince, you pass not;
Guards keep the door; the King your Father lives—

ARTAXERES
Ha!—if he lives, why lives he not to me?
Why am I thus shut out and banisht from him?
Why are my veins rich with his Royal blood?
Why did he give me Life if not to serve him?
Forbid me not to wait upon his Bed,
And watch his sickly slumbers, that my youth
May with its service glad his drooping age,
And his cold hand may bless me e're he dye.
Nay, be a Queen, and rob me of his Crown,
But let me keep my right to filial piety.

QUEEN
Well hast thou urg'd the specious name of Duty
To hide deform d Rebellion; Hast thou not
With thy false arts poyson'd his peoples Loyalty?
What meant thy pompous progress thro the Empire,
Thy vast profusion to the factious Nobles,
Whose interest sways the Croud, and stirs up Mutiny?
Why did thy haughty, fierce, disdainful Soul
Stoop to the meanest arts which catch the vulgar?
Herd with 'em, fawn upon 'em, and caress 'em;
Appeal to them, to them relate thy wrongs,
And make them Judges of thy Fathers Justice?
Thy cruel and unnatural lust of power
Have sunk thy Father more than all his years,
And made him wither in a green old age.

ARTAXERES

False all as hell: Nor had I arm'd my friends
But to defend that right.—

QUEEN

Dost thou not come,
Impatient of delay to hasten fate?
To bring that death, the lingering disease
Would only for a day or two defer.

ARTAXERES

Thear thee, and disdain thy little malice,
That dares to stain my virtue with a Crime.
It views with most abhorrence; but reproach
Is lost on thee, since Modesty with all
The Vertues that adorn thy Sex is fled.

QUEEN

Audacious Rebel!

ARTAXERES

Infamous Adultress!
Stain of my Fathers Bed, and of his Throne!

ARTABAN

Villain! thou ly'st! oh Madam give me way,
To the Queen, who holds him, drawing his Sword.
Whatever bars my fury calls me base,
Unworthy of the honor of your Son.

QUEEN

Hold Artaban! my honour suffers not
From his lewd breath, nor shall thy Sword prophane
With brawls or blood the reverence of this place,
To peace and sacred Majesty devoted.

ARTAXERES

Ha! who art thou?
To Artaban.

ARTABAN

The son of great Arsaces,

ARTAXERES

No! 'tis false! thy forging mother's damn'd contrivance.
Seek for thy Father in that plotting fellow,
The Hero's race disclaims thee. Why dost thou frown,

And knit thy boyish brow? Dost thou dare ought
Worthy the rank of the Divine Arsacides?
If so, come forth, break from that womans arms,
And meet me with thy good Sword like a man.

ARTABAN
Yes! Artaxerxes, yes! thou shalt be met:
The mighty Gods have held us in the balance,
And one of us is doom'd to sink for ever.
Nor can I bear a long delay of Fate,
But wish the great decision were ev'n now.
Proud and ambitious Prince, I dare like thee,
All that is great and glorious. Like thine,
Immortal thirst of Empire fires my soul,
My soul, which of superiour power impatient,
Disdains thy Eldership; therefore in Arms
Which give the noblest right to Kings) I will
To death dispute with thee the Throne of Cyrus.

ARTAXERES
Do this, and thou art worthy of my anger:
O energy divine of great Ambition.
That can inform the souls of beardless Boys,
And ripen 'em to Men in spight of Nature.
I tell thee, Boy, that Empire is a Cause,
For which the Gods might wage Immortal War.
Then let my soul exert her utmost vertue,
And think at least thou art Arsaces Son,
That the Idea o' thy fancy'd Father
May raise and animate thy leader Genius,
And make thee fit to meet my arm in Battel.

ARTABAN
Oh doubt not but my soul is charm'd with greatness,
So much it rivals even the joy of Knowledge
And Sacred Wisdom. What makes Gods divine,
But Power and Science infinite?
Hear only this; our Father, prest by age,
And a long train of Evils which that brings,
Languishes in the last Extremes of life:
Since thou wouldst blot my birth with base dishonour,
Be this my proof of filial piety,
While yet he lives cease we our enmity;
Nor let the hideous noise of War disturb
His parting Soul.

ARTAXERES
I take thee at thy word:

Let his remains of life be Peace betwixt us,
And after that let all our time be War.
Remember when we meet, since one must fall,
Who Conquers and Survives, Survives to Empire.

[Exeunt severally, **QUEEN** and **ARTABAN**, **ARTAXERES**, **MEMNON**. cum suis.

[Manent **MIRZA** and **MAGAS**.

MIRZA
Most fortunate Event! which gives us more
Than even our wishes could have askt. This Truce
Gives lucky opportunity for thinking;
'Twill lull these thoughtless Heroes to security.

MAGAS
Th' approaching Festival will more confirm it:
Of all those sacred times which heretofore
Religion has distinguisht from the rest,
And to the service of the Gods devoted,
This has been still most venerable held;
Among the vulgar, toil and labour ceases
With Chaplets crown'd, they dance to the shrill Pipe,
And in their Songs invoke those milder Deities,
That soften anxious life with peace and pleasure;
Slaves are enfranchis'd, and inveterate foes
Forget, or at the least suspend their hate,
And meet like friends. Pernicious discord seems
Out rooted from our more than Iron age:
The Gods are worship with unusual Reverence,
Since none, not ev'n our Kings, approach their Temples
With any mark of Wars destructive Rage,
But Sacrifice unarm'd.

MIRZA
A lucky thought
Is in my mind at once compleatly form'd,
Like Grecian Pallas in the head of Jove.
When Memnon, Artaxerxes, and their friends,
Shall, in obedience to the Holy Rites,
To morrow at the Altar bow unarm'd,
Orchanes with a party of the Guards,
Who in my Palace shall this night be plac'd,
May at that private door which opens into
The Temple, rush at once, and seize 'em all.
The heads once safe, the mean and heartless Crowd
With ease may be disperst.

MAGAS

What you propose
Wears a successful face, were it as innocent:
An act of such outrageous prophanation,
May shock the thoughts ev'n of our closest friends,
And make 'em start from an abhorr'd alliance,
That draws the vengeance of the Gods upon 'em.

MIRZA

Art thou the first to start a doubt like that?
Art thou (who dost inspire their Oracles,
And teach 'em to deceive the easie Crowd
In doubtful phrase) afraid of thy own Gods?
In every change they were on thy side still,
And sure they will not leave thee now for trifles.
The Gods shall certainly befriend our Cause,
At least not be our foes, nor will they leave
Their happy seats (where free from care and pain,
Blest in themselves alone, of man regardless,
They loll serene in Everlasting Ease)
To mind the trivial business of our world.

MAGAS

But more I fear the Superstitious Vulgar,
Who tho unknowing what Religion means,
Yet nothing moves 'em more than zealous rage
For its defence, when they believe it violated.

MIRZA

I was to blame to tax the Priest with scruples,
Or think his care of Interest was his Conscience.
[Aside.
My Caution shall obviate all thy fears;
We will give out that they themselves design'd
To fire the Temple, and then kill the King.
No matter tho it seem not very probable,
More monstrous tales have oft amus'd the vulgar.

MAGAS

I yield to your direction, and to strengthen
The Enterprize, will secretly dispose
A party of my own within the Temple,
To joyn with yours.

MIRZA

It joys my heart to think
That I shall glut my vengeance on this Memnon:
That I shall see him strive in vain, and Curse

The happy fraud that caught him. Like a Lyon,
Who long has reign'd the terror of the Woods,
And dar'd the boldest Huntsman to the Combat;
Till catcht at length within some hidden snare,
With soaming Jaws he bites the Toils that hold him,
And roars and rowls his fiery eyes in vain;
While the surrounding Swains at pleasure wound him,
And make his death their sport.
Thus Wit still gets the mastery o're Courage.
Long time unmatcht in War the Hero shone,
And mighty Fame in fields of Battel won;
Till one fine project of the Statesman's Brain
Bereaves him of the spoyls his Arms did gain,
And renders all his boasted prowess vain.

[Exeunt.

ACT III

SCENE I. A Garden Belonging to Mirza's Palace

CLEONE is discover'd lying on a bank of Flowers, attending.

SONG, [by B. Stote, Esq]
Upon a shady Bank repos'd,
Philanthe, amorous, young, and fair,
Sighing to the Groves, disclos'd
The story of her Care.
The Vocal Groves give some relief,
While they her notes return,
The Waters murmur o're her grief,
And [.....] seems to mourn.
A Swain that heard the Nymph complain,
In pity of the fair,
Thus kindly strove to Cure her pain,
And Ease her mind of Care.
Tis just that Love should give you rest,
From Love your Torments came;
Take that warm Cordial to your breast,
And meet a kinder flame.
How wretched must the woman prove,
Beware, fair Nymph, beware,
Whose folly scorns anothers Love,
And Courts her own Despair.

CLEONE

Oh Love! thou bane of an unhappy Maid!
Still art thou busie at my panting heart?
Still dost thou melt my Soul with thy soft Images,
And make my ruine pleasing? fondly I try
By gales of Sighs and Floods of streaming Tears,
To vent my sorrows, and asswage my passions.
Still fresh supplies renew th' exhausted stores.
Love reigns my Tyrant, to himself alone
He vindicates the Empire of my breast,
And banishes all thoughts of joy for ever.

BELIZA

Why are you still thus Cruel to your self?
Why do you feed and cherish the disease,
That preys on your dear life? how can you hope
To find a Cure for Love in solitude?
Why rather chuse you not to shine at Court?
And in a thousand gay diversions there,
To lose the memory of this wretched passion?

CLEONE

Alas! Beliza, thou hast never known
The fatal power of a resistless Love;
Like that avenging guilt that haunts the Impious,
In vain we hope by flying to avoid it,
In Courts and Temples it pursues us still,
And in the loudest clamours will be heard:
It grows a part of us, lives in our blood,
And every beating pulse proclaims its force.
Oh! think not then that I can shun my self;
The Grave can only hide me from my sorrows.

BELIZA

Allow me then at least to share your griefs,
Companions in misfortunes make 'em less;
And I could suffer much to make you easie.

CLEONE

Sit by me, gentle Maid, and while I tell
A wretched tale of unregarded Love,
If thou in kind compassion of my woes,
Shalt sigh or shed a tear for my mishap,
My grateful eyes shall pay it back with interest.
Help me to rail at my too easie heart,
That rashly entertain'd this fatal guest:
And you, my eyes! why were you still impatient
Of any other sight but Artaxerxes?
Why did you make my womans heart acquainted

With all the thousand graces and perfections,
That dress the lovely Hero up for Conquest?

BELIZA
Had you oppos'd this passion in its infancy,
E're time had given it strength, it might have dy'd.

CLEONE
That was the fatal Error that undid me:
My Virgin thoughts, and unexperienc'd Innocence,
Found not the danger till it was too late.
And tho when first I saw the charming Prince,
I felt a pleasing motion at my heart,
Short breathing sighs heav'd in my panting breast,
The mounting blood flusht in my glowing face,
And dy'd my cheeks with more than usual blushes,
I thought him sure the wonder of his kind,
And wisht my fate had given me such a Brother:
Yet knew not that I lov'd, but thought that all
Like me, beheld and blest him for his Excellence.

BELIZA
Sure never hopeless Maid was curst before
With such a wretched passion; all the Gods
Join to oppose your happiness; 'tis said
This day the Prince shall wed the fair Amestris.

CLEONE
No, my Beliza, I have never known
The pleasing thoughts of hope: certain despair
Was born at once, and with my love encreas'd.

BELIZA
Think you the Prince has e're perceiv'd your thoughts?

CLEONE
Forbid it all ye chaster powers, that favour
The modesty and Innocence of Maids:
No, till my death no other breast but thine
Shall e're participate the fatal secret.
O could I think that he had ever known
My hidden flame, shame and confusion
Would force my Virgin soul to leave her mansion,
And certain Death ensue.
Thou name'st the fair Amestris, didst thou not?

BELIZA
Madam, I did.

CLEONE

I envy not her happiness;
Tho sure few of our Sex are blest like her
In such a Godlike Lord.
Would I had been a man!
With honour then I might have sought his friendship!
Perhaps from long experience of my faith,
He might have lov'd me better than the rest.
Amidst the dangers of the horrid War,
Still had I been the nearest to his side;
In Courts and Triumphs still had shar'd his joys,
Or when the sportful Chace had call'd us forth,
Together had we cheer'd our foaming Steeds,
Together prest the Savage o're the plain.
And when o're-labour'd with the pleasing toil,
Stretcht on the verdant soil had slept together.
But whither does my roving fancy wander?
These are the sick dreams of fantastick love.
So in a Calenture, the Sea-man fancies
Green Fields and Flowry Meadows on the Ocean,
Till leaping in, the wretch is lost for ever.

BELIZA

Try but the Common Remedies of Love,
And let a second flame expel the first.

CLEONE

Impossible; as well thou mayst imagine,
When thou complainst of heat at scorching noon,
Another Sun shall rise to shine more kindly.
Believe me, my Beliza, I am grown
So fond of the delusion that has charm'd me,
I hate the officious hand that offers cure.

BELIZA

Madam, Prince Artaban.

CLEONE

My cruel Stars
Do ye then envy me my very solitude;
But death, the wretches only remedy,
Shall hide me from your hated Light for ever.

[Enter **ARTABAN**.

ARTABAN

Ah! Lovely Mourner, still! still wilt thou blast

My eager Love with unauspicious Tears?
When at thy Feet I kneel, and sue for pity,
Or justly of thy cold regards complain,
Still wilt thou only answer me with sighs?

CLEONE
Alas! my Lord, what answer can I give?
If still I entertain you with my grief,
Pity the temper of a wretched Maid,
By [.....] sad and born the child of sorrow.
In vain you ask for happiness from me,
Who want it for my self.

ARTABAN
Can blooming Youth,
And Virgin Innocence, that knows not guilt,
Know any cause for grief?

CLEONE
Do but survey
The miserable state of humane kind,
Where wretches are the general Encrease,
And tell me if there be not cause for grief

ARTAXERES
Such thoughts as these, my fair Philosopher,
Inhabit wrinkled cheeks, and hollow eyes;
The marks which years set on the wither'd Sage;
The gentle Goddess Nature wisely has
Alotted other cares for youth and beauty.
The God of Love stands ready with his Torch
To light it at thy eyes, but still in vain,
For e re the slame can catch, 'tis drown'd in tears.

CLEONE
Oh! name not Love, the worst of all misfortunes,
The common ruin of my easie Sex,
Which I have sworn for ever to avoid,
In memory of all those hapless Maids,
That Love has plung'd in unexampled woes.

ARTABAN
For bear to argue, with that Angel face,
Against the passion thou wert form'd to raise.
Alas! thy frozen heart has only known
Love in Reverse, not tasted of its joys;
The wishes, soft desires, and pleasing pains,
That centre all in most extatick bliss.

Oh, lovely Maid, mis-spend no more that treasure
Of Youth and Charms, which lavish Nature gives;
The Paphian Goddess frowns at thy delay;
By her fair self and by her Son she swears,
Thy Beauties are devoted to her service.
Now! now she shoots her fires into my breast,
She urges my desires, and bids me seize thee,

[Taking her hand, and kissing it.

And bear thee as a Victim to her Altar,
Then offer up ten thousand thousand joys,
As an amends for all thy former coldness.

CLEONE
Forbear, my Lord; or I must swear to fly
For ever from your sight.

ARTABAN
Why dost thou frown?
And damp the rising joy within my breast?
Art thou resolv'd to force thy gentle nature,
Compassionate to all the World beside,
And only to me cruel? Shall my vows,
Thy Fathers intercession all be vain?

CLEONE
Why do you urge my Fathers fatal power,
To Curse you with a sad unlucky Bride?
Cast round your eyes on our gay Eastern Courts,
Where smiling Beauties, born to better fates,
Give joy to the beholders.
There bless some happy Princess with your vows,
And leave the poor Cleone to her sorrows.

ARTABAN
What Queens are those, of most celestial form,
Whose Charms can drive thy Image from my heart?
Oh were they cast in Natures fairest mold,
Brighter than Cynthia's shining train of Stars,
Kind as the softest she that ever claspt
Her Lover, when the Bridal night was past;
I swear I would prefer thee, O Cleone
With all thy scorn and cold indifference,
Would choose to languish and to dye for thee,
Much rather than be blest, and live for them.

CLEONE

Oh Prince, it is too much; nor am I worthy
The honour of your passion, since 'tis fixt
By certain and unalterable fate,
That I can never yield you a return:
My thoughts are all to chaste Diana vow'd,
And I have sworn to die her Virgin Votary.

ARTABAN
Impossible! thou canst not give away
Mine and thy Fathers right, ev'n to the Gods;
Diana will disown the unjust donation,
Nor favour such an injury to Love.
To every power divine I will appeal,
Nor shall thy Beauty bribe 'em to be partial:
Their Altars now expect us; Come, fair Saint,
And if thou wilt abide their righteous doom,
Their Justice must decree my happiness,
Reward my sufferings, and my flame approve,
For they themselves have felt the pow'r of Love.

[Exeunt.

SCENE II. The Temple of the Sun

Enter **ARTAXERES**, **AMESTRIS**, and **ATTENDANTS**.

ARTAXERES
'Tis done! 'Tis done! oh let me find some way
To tell the mighty joy that fills my breast,
Lest I grow mad with height of furious bliss.
The holy Priest has ty'd the sacred knot,
And my Amestris now is all my own.
Oh thou soft Charmer! thou excelling Sweetness!
Why art thou not transported all like me:
I swear thou dost not love thy Artaxerxes,
If thou art calm in this excess of happiness.

AMESTRIS
Alas! my Lord! my panting heart yet trembles
In vast suspence between unruly joys
And chilling fears; somewhat methinks there is
That checks my soul, and says I was too bold
To quit the pleasures of my Virgin state,
To barter 'em for cares and anxious love.

ARTAXERES

These are the fears which wait on every Bride,
And only serve for preludes to her joys;
Short sighs, and all those motions of thy heart,
Are Nature's call, and kindle warm desires;
Soon as the friendly Goddess of the night,
Shall draw her vail of darkness o're thy blushes,
These little cold unnecessary doubts,
Shall fly the circle of my folding arms:
And when I press thee trembling to my bosom,
Thou shalt confess (if there be room for words,
Or ev'n for thoughts) that all those thoughts are bliss.

AMESTRIS

Yet surely mine are more than common fears;
For oh! my Prince, when my foreboding heart
Surveys the uncertain state of humane joys,
How secretly the malice of our fate
Unseen pursues, and often blasts our happiness
In full security; I justly dread,
Lest death or parting, or some unseen accident,
Much worse, if possible, than each of these,
Should curse us more than ever we were blest.

ARTAXERES

Doubt not the Gods, my Fair! whose righteous power
Shall favour and protect our vertuous Loves.
If still thou apprehendst approaching danger,
Let us make haste, and snatch th' uncertain joy,
While fate is in our power.
Now let us start, and give a loose to Love,
Feast ev'ry sence with most luxurious pleasure,
Improve our minutes, make 'em more than years,
Than ages, and ev'n live the life of Gods:
Of after this, death or ill fortune comes,
[.....] cannot injure us, since we already
Have liv'd, and been before-hand with our fate.

AMESTRIS

Oh let me ease at once my tender heart,
And tell my dearest Lord my worst of fears:
There is an ill which more than death I dread;
Would you, by time and long fruition sated,
Grow faithless, and forget the lost Amestris;
Forget that Everlasting truth you vow'd,
Tho sure I should not publickly complain
Nor to the Gods accuse my perjur'd Prince,
Yet my soft soul would sink beneath the weight.
I should grow mad, and curse my very being,

And wish I ne're had been, or not been lov'd.

ARTAXERES
Dost thou?—when every happier Star shines for us,
And with propitious Influence gilds our fortune,
Dost thou invent fantastick forms of danger,
And fright thy soul with things that are Impossible?
Now by the Potent God of Love, I swear
I will have ample vengeance for thy doubts.
My soft complaining Fair, shalt thou not pay me
In Joys too fierce for thought, for these suspicions.
The bands which hold our Love are knit by fate,
Nor shall decaying time or nature loose 'em.
Beyond the limits of the silent Grave,
Love shall survive, immortal as our beings,
And when at once we climb yon azure Skies,
We will be shown to all the blest above,
For the most constant pair that e're deserv'd
To mingle with their Stars.

AMESTRIS
'Tis true! 'tis true!
Nor ought I to suspect thee, O my Hero!
The Gods have form'd thee for the nearest pattern
Of their own excellence and perfect truth.
Oh let me sink upon thy gentle bosome,
And blushing tell how greatly I am blest.
Forgive me Modesty, if here I vow
That all the pleasures of my Virgin state
Were poor and trifling to the present rapture.
A gentle warmth invades my glowing breast,
And while I fondly gaze upon thy face,
Ev'n thought is lost in exquisite delight.

ARTAXERES
Oh thou delicious perfect Angel Woman!
Thou art too much for mortal sence to bear:
The Vernal bloom and fragrancy of Spices
Wafted by gentle winds, are not like thee.
From thee, as from the Cyprian Queen of Love,
Ambrosial odours flow, my every faculty
Is charm'd by thee, and drinks Immortal pleasure.
Oh glorious God of day fly swiftly forward,
And to thy Sisters rule resign the world:
Nor haste to rise again, but let the night
Long bless me with her stay; that thy return
At morn may find me happiest of my kind.

[Enter **MEMNON**.

My Father! is there an Increase of joy?
What can ye give, ye Gods, to make it more?

MEMNON
Ye Blessings of my age: whom when I view,
The memory of former woes is lost.
Oh Prince! well has this glorious day repay'd
My youth and blood spent in Arsaces service.
Nor had the Gods indulg'd my vainest wishes,
Durst I have askt for such a Son as you are.
But I am roughly bred, in words unknowing,
Nor can I phrase my speech in apt expression,
To tell how much I love and honour you.
Might I but live to fight one Battel for you,
Tho with my Life I bought the Victory,
Tho my old batter'd trunk were hew'd to pieces,
And scatter'd o're the field, yet should I bless
My fate, and think my years wound up with honour.

ARTAXERES
Doubt not, my noble Father, but even yet
A large remain of Glory is behind.
When Civil discord shall be reconcil'd,
And all the noise of Faction husht to Peace,
Rough Greece, alike in Arts and Arms severe,
No more shall brand the Persian name with softness.
Athens and Sparta wondring shall behold us,
Strict in our discipline, undaunted, patient
Of Wars stern toil, and dread our hostile vertue.
Those stubborn Commonwealths, that proudly dare
Disdain the glorious Monarchs of the East,
Shall pay their homage to the Throne of Cyrus.
And when with Lawrels cover'd we return,
My Love shall meet, and smiling bless our triumph,
While at her feet I lay the Scepters of the world.

MEMNON
Oh glorious theme! by heaven it fires my age,
And kindles youth again in my cold veins.

ARTAXERES
Ha! Mirza and the Queen! retire my fair,
Ungentle hate and brawling rage shall not
Disturb the peace, to which this happy day
Is doubly sacred. Forward, to the Altar.

[Exeunt **ARTAXERXES**, **ARMESTRIS**, **MEMNON**, and **ATTENDANTS**.

[Enter at the other door, **QUEEN**, **MIRZA**, and **ATTENDANTS**.

MIRZA
All are dispos'd, and fate but waits our orders
For a deciding blow.

QUEEN
Your Caution was
Both wise and faithful, not to trust my Son
Too rashly with a secret of this nature.
The youth, tho great of soul, and fond of glory,
Yet leans to the fantastick rules of Honour,
Would hesitate at such an act as this,
Tho future Empire should depend upon it.

MIRZA
When time shall add experience to that knowledge,
With which his early youth is richly fraught,
He'll be convinc'd that only Fools would lose
A Crown for notionary Principles.
Honour is the unthinking Souldier's boast,
Whose dull head cannot reach those finer arts,
By which Mankind is govern'd.

QUEEN
And yet it gives a lustre to the Great,
And Makes the Croud adore 'em.

MIRZA
Your Son shall reap
The whole advantage, while we bear the guilt:
You, Madam, when the sacred Hymns are finisht,
Must with the Prince retire; our foes when seiz'd,
Within the Temple may be best secur'd,
Till you dispose their fare.

QUEEN
The Rites attend us,
Solemn Musick is heard.
This day my Son is Monarch of the East.

MIRZA
Lend us, ye Gods, your Temples but this day,
You shall be paid with Ages of devotion,
And after this for ever undisturb'd,
Brood o're your smoaking Altars.

[Exeunt **QUEEN**, **MIRZA**, and **ATTENDANTS**.

The Scene opening shews the Altar of the Sun, **MAGAS** and several other **PRIESTS** attending.

Solemn Musick is heard; then Enter on one side **MEMMON**, **ARTAXERXES**, **AMESTRIS**, and **ATTENDANTS**, on the other side the **QUEEN**, **MIRZA**, **ARTABAN**, **CLEONE**, **CLEANTHES**, and **ATTENDANTS**; they all bow towards the Altar, and then range themselves on each side of the Stage, while the following Hymn is perform'd in Parts, and Chorus by the **PRIESTS**.

HYMN to the Sun [by W. Shippen. Esq]
Hail Light, that doubly glads our sphere,
Glory and Triumph of the year!
Hail Festival for ever blest,
By the adoring ravisht East!
Hail Mithras, mighty Deity!
For Fire and Air, and Earth and Sea,
From thee their origin derive,
Motion and Form from thee receive.
When Matter yet unacted lay,
No sooner thou infus'd thy ray,
But the dull mass its pow'r obey'd,
But an harmonious World was made.
Which still, when thou withdrawst thy beams,
An undistinguisht Chaos seems;
For what are objects without sight?
Or vision when involv'd in night?
Night is an universal Grave,
Where things but doubtful beings have,
Till them thy beams illuminate,
And as it were again create.

CHORUS, &c.
Hail source of immaterial fire,
That ne're begun, can ne're expire,
Whose Orh, with streaming Glories fraught,
Dazles the ken of human thought!
All the dependant Spheres above,
By thy direction shine and move.
All purer beings here below,
From thy immediate Essence flow.
What is the Soul of man but light,
Drawn down from thy transcendent height?
What but an Intellectual beam?

A spark of thy immortal flame?
For as thou rulest with gladsome rays
The greater world, so this the less,
And like thy own diffusive Soul,
Shoots life and vigour thro the whole.
Since then from thee at first it came,
To thee, tho clogg d, it points its flame,
And conscious of superiour birth,
Despises this unkindred Earth.

CHORUS, &c.
Hail Orosmades, Pow'r Divine!
Permits us to approach thy shrine,
Permit thy Votartes to raise
Their grateful voices to thy praise.
Thou art the Father of our Kings,
The stem whence their high lineage springs,
The Sov'reign Lord that does maintain
Their uncontroul'd and boundless Reign.
O then assist thy drooping Son,
Who long has grac't our Persian Throne!
O may he yet extend his sway!
We yet Arsaces Rule obey!
Let thy vitiality impart
New Spirits to his fainting Heart;
Let him like thee (from whom he sprung)
Be ever Active, ever Young.

CHORUS, &c.

[When the Musick is ended **MEMMON**, **ARTAXERXES**, &c. **QUEEN**, **ARTABAN**, &c. go off as they Enter'd, severally: only **MIRZA** comes forward and the Scene shuts; he looks after **AMESTRIS** going out, and then speaks.

MIRZA
What means this foreign warmth within my Breast?
Is this a time for any thought but Vengeance?
That fatal Beauty dazles my weak Sense,
And blasts the resolution of my Soul:
My Eyes in contradiction to my purpose,
Still bent to her, and drunk the Poyson in;
While I stood stupid in suspence of thought.
And now like Oyl my flaming Spirits blaze,
My Arteries, my Heart, my Brain is scortch't,
And I am all one fury. Feeble Mirza!
Can'st thou give way to dotage, and become
The jest of Fools? No! 'tis Impossible:
Revenge shall rouse, and with her Iron whips

Lash sorth this lazy Ague from my Blood,
This Malady of Girls. Remember Statesman,
Thy Fate and future Fortunes now are forming,
And Summon all thy Counsels to their Aid;
Ev'n thy whole Soul. It wo'not be; Amestris
Still rises uppermost in all my thoughts,
The Master piece of Nature. The Boy God
Laughs at my Rage, and triumphs o're my Folly.
Ha! by the Gods 'tis doing! Now my Stars
A tumultuous noise is heard.
Be kind and make me Master of my wish at once.
A tumultuous noise is heard.

[Enter **MAGAS**.

But see the Priest! Why dost thou stare and tremble,
Have we succeeded, say; and ease my Fears.

MAGAS
My Soul is pierc't with Horror! Every God
Seems from his shrine to threaten us with Vengeance.
The Temple reels and all its pond'rous Roof
Nods at the Prophanation.

MIRZA
Base and fearful!
How can thy wretched Soul conceive such Monsters?
Can'st thou who would'st be great be Superstitious?
But 'tis the Cowards Vice. Say; are our Enemies secur'd?

MAGAS
They are; the Prince, Old Memnon and his Daughter
Are in Orchanes hands, only Tigranes
With some of Lesser note are fled.

MIRZA
No matter:
These are the Soul, the rest a lifeless Mass,
Not worth our Apprehension.

MAGAS
Will you stay,
To meet the furious Thunder of their Rage?

MIRZA
I will; thou may'st retire and summon back.
Thy scatter'd Spirits; Let not the Crowd see
Thy Fears, 'twill make the Vile and Cheap among 'em

[Exit **MAGAS**.

[Enter **ARTAXERXES**, **MEMNON** and **AMESTRIS**, PRISONERS, **ORCHANES** and **GUARDS**.

ARTAXERES
Slave! Villain! Answer, say how hast thou dar'd
To do this Insolence?—

ORCHANES
I know my orders
Which from the Queen my Mistress I receiv'd,
Who will avow her own Authority.

ARTAXERES
Ha! from the Queen! She durst not! 'tis Impossible!
'Tis Sacriledge! 'tis Treason! 'tis Damnation.
Am I not Artaxerxes? Born to Empire,
The next degree to God's. Oh thou bright Sun!
That roul'st above the Object of our Worship.
Can'st thou behold and not avenge thy Race?
Thy injur'd Race? If I could ought admit
Unworthy of thy great Original.
Let me be doom'd to fall this Villain's Slave,
If not!—Why am I made the scorn of Wretches?
So much below me that they hardly share
The Common priviledge of Kind; but are
As Beasts to Men.—

MEMNON
See where the Master Villain stands! unmov'd
And harden'd in Impiety, he laughs
At the fictitious Justice of the God's,
And thinks their Thunder has not Wings to reach him;
but know the Joy thy Triumph brings is short,
My Fate (if the God's govern) or at least
My Mind's beyond thy reach, and scorns thy Malice.

MIRZA
Dull valiant Fool thy Ruin is the least
The most ignoble Triumph of my Wit.
Cleander's
Blood asks for substantial Vengeance,
And when the thought that labours in my Breast
Appears in Action, thou shalt know the cause
Why I remain to view thy hated Face,
That blasts me with its Presence; thou shalt know it
And Curse thy self, Curse the ill-omen'd day

That gave the Birth, renouncing all the God's,
Thy self of them renounc'd, shal't sink to Hell
In bitterest Pangs and mingle with the furies.

MEMNON
Unhallow'd Dog, thou ly'st! The utmost force
Of all thy study'd Malice cannot move me
To any act that misbecomes my Courage,
And if the God's in tryal of my Virtue
Can yield my Life up to thy Hangman's Mercy;
I le shew thee with what ease the Brave and Honest
Can put off Life till thou shal't damn thy Arts,
Thy wretched Arts, and Impotence of Malice.

MIRZA
Rest well assur'd, thou shalt have cause to try
The Philosophick sorce of Passive Vertue.

ARTAXERES
Oh death to Greatness! Can we fall so low
To be the slavish Objects of his Mirth?
Shall my just Rage and violated Honour
Play the Buffoon and Minister to laughter?
Down, down my swelling Heart, hide thy Resentments,
Nor prostitute the ruffled Majesty
Of injur'd Princes to the gazing Crow'd,
My Face shall learn to cover the Emotion
My wounded Soul endures. Ha! my Amestris!
My Love! my Royal Bride! the spoiler Grief
Defaces every Feature, like the Deluge
That ras't the Beauties of the first Creation;
I cannot bear it! Villains give me way!

[He breaks from the **GUARDS** that hold him and catches hold of **AMESTRIS**.

Oh let me hold thee in my throbbing Bosom,
And strive to hide thy Sorrows from my sight,
I cannot see thy Griefs; and yet I want
The power to bring Relief.

AMESTRIS
Ah! no my Prince!
There are no remedies for Ills like ours;
My helpless Sex by nature stands expos'd
To all the Wrongs and Injuries of Fortune,
Defenceless in my self, you were my resuge,
You are my Lord, to whom should I Complain,
Since you cannot redress me: were you not

The Honour, Joy, and Safety of Amestris?
For you alone I liv'd, with you alone
I could be happy, oh my Artaxerxes!
One influence guides our Consenting Stars,
And still together are we Blest or Curst.

MIRZA
With a malignant Joy my Ears drink in,
Hear cach Harmonious accent every glance,
Goes to my Heart and stirs, alternate Motions
Of Heat and Cold, a lazy pleasure now
Thrills all my Veins, anon Desire grows hot,
And my old Sinews shrink before the Flame.

ARTAXERES
Go on! And Charm me with thy Angels Voice,
Sooth and asswage the Fury in my Breast,
That urges me to unbecoming Passion,
My Rage grows cool amidst thy soft Complainings,
And though thou talk'st of Woes, of Death and Ruin,
'Tis Heaven to hear thee.

AMESTRIS
Since this is all our wretched Consolation,
Let us indulge our Grief, 'till by long use,
It grows Habitual, and we lose the pain.
Here, on the Marble Pavement will we sit,
Thy Head upon my Breast; and if remembrance
Of Cruel Wrongs, shall vex thy noble Heart,
The Murmur of my Sighs shall Charm the Tumult,
And Fate shall fiind us Calm; nor will the Gods,
Who here inhabit and behold our Sufferings,
Delay to end our Woes in Immortality.

ARTAXERES
Ha! say'st thou? God's! Yes certain there are God's,
To whom my Youth with Reverence still has bow'd,
Whose Care and Providence are Virtues Guard,
Think then my fair they have not made us great,
And like themselves for miserable ends.

MIRZA
God's might behold her and forget their Wisdom,
[Aside.
But I delay too long! Orchanes lend thy Ear.

MEMNON
My Children! you were still my Joy and Happiness.

[**MIRZA** whispers **ORCHANES**, and Exit.

Why am I made your Curse? this hated Head
To death devoted, has involv'd your Innocence
In my Destruction.

[**GUARDS** lay hold on **ARTAXERXES** and **AMESTRIS**.

AMESTRIS
Alas, my Father!—

ARTAXERES
Barbarous Dogs! what mean you?

ORCHANES
Convey the Lady to Lord Mirza's Palace,
'Tis the Queen's will she shall be there confin'd.

ARTAXERES
Thou can'st not mean so damn'd a Villany!
Thou dar'st not! shal't not part us! Fate cannot do it!

MEMNON
Cursed Old Age, why have I liv'd to see this?

ORCHANES
Force 'em asunder.

ARTAXERES
Hew off my Limbs ye Dogs! I will not lose 'em—
Oh Devils! Death and Furies! my Wife! my lov'd Amestris!—

AMESTRIS
My Lord! my Husband!—

[**ORCHANES** and one party of the **GUARDS** force **ARTAXERXES** and **MEMNON** off one way, and the other party bears **AMESTRIS** another.

[Re-enter **MIRZA**.

MIRZA
This was most noble Mischief! it stung home,
'Twas Luxury of Vengeance!—'twas not ill
To keep aloof; these boistorous Beasts have Paws,
And might have scratch't: The Wise should not allow
A possibility to Fortunes Malice.
Now to the rest; this Prince! this Husband! dies:

To Morrows dawn brings his and Memnon's Fate.
This Night let 'em dispair, and Bann, and Rage,
And to the wooden Deities within,
Tell frantick Tales; my Hours shall pass more pleasingly;
If Love, (which yet I know not,) can give Pleasure.
Love! What is Love? the Passion of a Boy,
That spends his time in Laziness and Sonnets:
Lust is the Appetite of Man; and shall
Be sated, till it loath the cloying Banquet.
The Wise are by Human frailty,
To tast these Pleasures, but not dwell upon 'em;
They marr and dull the faculty of thinking;
One Night I safely may indulge in Riot,
'Tis Politick lewdness, and Assists my Vengeance;
I will grow Young, and surfeit on her Charms,
Her luscious Sweets; then rising from her Arms,
The nauseous, momentary Joy forget,
And be my self again; again be Wise and Great.

[Exit **MIRZA**.

ACT IV

SCENE I. The Palace

Enter **ARTABAN** and **CLEANTHES**.

ARTABAN
'Tis Base and Impious! where are the
Ties shall keep Mankind in Order? if Religion
And publick Faith be Violated; 'Tis an Injury
That beards both Gods and Men; and dares their Justice.

CLEANTHES
The fearful Crowd already take the Alarm,
Break off their Solemn Sports, their Songs and Dances,
And wildly in tumultuous Consort joyn;
Mischief and Danger sits in every Face,
And while they dread the Anger of the Gods,
The Wise who know th' Effects of Popular Fury,
From them expect that Vengeance which they Fear.

ARTABAN
The Sacred Power of Majesty, which should
Forbid, owns and protects the Violence;
It must not, shall not be; Who steals a Crown

By Arts like these, wears it unworthily.

CLEANTHES
The Queen your Mother, Sir! She will expect
You should approve that Act her Power has done.

ARTABAN
I'll meet her as I ought, and show my self
Worthy the Noble Rivalship of Empire.

[Enter the **QUEEN**, **MIRZA** and **ATTENDANTS**.

QUEEN
My Son, I come to Joy you of a Crown
And Glory certain now, your Fate at length,
Has Master'd that Malignant Influence
With which it struggl'd long: You are a King,
The greatest that our Eastern World beholds,
And tho' my Widow'd Bed be Cause for Grief,
Yet for thy Sake, my Son, I joy to say,
Arsaces is no more.

ARTABAN
'Twere vain and foolish,
To Mourn his Death with Ceremonious Sorrow;
For tho' he died the Greatest of our Race,
Yet since decaying Age had sunk him low
And all the Native Majesty was lost,
'Twas time the Soul should seek for Immortality,
And leave the weary Body to Enjoy
An Honourable Rest from Care and Sickness:
Peace to his Ashes, and Eternal Fame
Dwell with his Memory, while we who Live
Look back with Emulation on his Greatness,
And with Laborious Steps strive to Ascend
That Height where once he sat.

QUEEN
Thou hast already
Attain'd the lofty Summit of his Glory;
His Throne expects thee but to sit and fill it.

ARTABAN
No, Madam, when the Gods chuse worthy Subjects
On whom to place such Greatness, they surround
The Glorious Prize with Toil and thorny Danger,
And bid the Man who would be Great, Dare greatly.
Be it for dull Elder Brothers to Possess

Without deserving; Mine's a Nobler Claim,
Nor will I Tast the godlike Joys of Power,
Till Men and Gods with Justice shall confess
'Tis barely the Reward of what I meant.

QUEEN
What means my Son?

ARTABAN
To Wrestle for a Crown!

QUEEN
With what fantastick Shadow wouldst thou strive?
The Haughty Rival of thy Hopes is fallen,
He lives indeed, but 'tis to Grace thy Triumph,
And Bow before thee; then be swept away
Like the remembrance of an Idle Dream,
Which tho' of Yesternight, is now forgotten.

ARTABAN
It greives me much to say, my Royal Mother,
I cannot take a Crown upon these Terms
Tho' even from your Hands: The Conscious Virtue
That witnesses within my Breast for Glory,
Points me to Greatness by the Paths of Honour,
And urges me to do as a King ought,
That would not wear his Purple as the Gift
Of impious Treachery and base Deceit.

QUEEN
Amazement turns my Senses! Or I Dream!
For sure thou canst not mean so poor a folly.
Hast thou been bred in the Wise Arts of Empire?
Been early taught to know the Worth of Power?
And would'st thou loose the Golden Opportunity
With which thy Fortune Courts thee for a Notion?
An Empty sound of Virtue? a dry Maxim
Which Pedants have devis'd for Boys to Canvas?
Can my Son think so meanly? Go set free
(Since Honour bids) this Lordly Elder Brother
Bow like a Slave before him, wait his Pleasures,
And live a dependant on his scanty Pension;
He may reward thy servile Loyalty,
And make thee ruler of some petty Province
In recompence of Royalty giv'n up.

ARTABAN
No! (tho' I must confess I would not hold him

Caught in a Villains Snare, nor do a Murther
Unworthy of a Hang-man) yet to death
I still defie him as my Mortal Foe,
And fince my Father's Fate dissolves that Truce,
To which I stood ingag'd; 'tis War again.
Amid'st the steely Squadrons will I seek
This haughty Brother, by his Friends surrounded
And back't with all th' Advantages of his Birth,
Then bravely prove upon him with my Sword;
He falsely brands me for a bookish Coward,
That Natures Error only gave him Preference,
Since Fate mean't me the King.

QUEEN
A Mothers Care is watchful for thy safety,
Else wer't thou lost, thou honourable Fool;
Long might'st thou vainly hunt in Bloody Fields;
For that Advantage which thy willing Fortune
Now reaches to thy hands: In Battles with
Uncertain Wings the wavering Goddess flys,
And [.....] with partial hand bestows her Favour
On Fools and thick Scull'd Heroes; seize her now
While she is thine, or she is lost for Ever.

ARTABAN
No matter, Let her fly; the Eagle Virtue
Shall [.....] beyond her and command her flight;
[.....] not my Mistress but my Slave.
[.....] reads the Name of Artaban
[.....] of Empire, shall not blush
To think I plotted with a Knavish Priest,
The Scandal of his venerable Function
And mark of the God's Vengeance, to betray
[.....] my Enemy; as if being Conscious
Of lesser worth, and of unequal Courage;
I durst not fairly strive with him for Greatness.
[.....] abborr'd and Impious Treachery
[.....] die, unknown to future Ages;
[.....] our Shame must be deliver'd down
[.....] all the Kingly hopes that fire my Soul,
[.....] shall not pass without a brand of Punishment.

QUEEN
'Tis wondrous well! Young Man you king rarely
You mean to be renown'd for early Justice,
And mark your Ostentacious Love of Virtue,
Ev'n in their Bloods, who lift up you to Power;
Perhaps we too, our self must be Arraign'd

Before your puny Bar, and feel your Ax;
'Twill be a Noble Subject for your Praise,
And yield much Matter to declaiming Flatterers.

ARTABAN
You, Madam, are my Mother, Nature blinds me,
And bids me see no Faults in her that bore me,
These other Slaves that dare—

QUEEN
May be Immortal,
For ought that thou Can'st do to cause their fate,
Is not thy Power the Creature of my Favour,
Which in precarious wise on me depending,
Exists by my Concurrence to its being?
Mistaken Youth! whose giddy Brain, Ambition
Has like the fume of drunken Vapours turn'd;
Think'st thou that I whose Soul was form'd for Sway,
Would lay the Golden Reins of Empire down?
Or trust 'em to the guidance of a Boy?
Who shall dispose of me, or those that serve me,
According to the dictates of Old Morals,
His bearded Tutor gleans from musty Authors.

ARTABAN
Nay then 'tis time I should Assert my self,
And tho' you gave me Birth; Yet from the Gods
(Who made my Father be as he was, Royal,
And stamp't the mark of Greatness on my Soul;)
I Claim my Right to Empire; may I sell
Vile and forgotten if I Ever own
Any Superiour Being but those God's.

QUEEN
Thou rav'st! and hast forgot me.

ARTABAN
No, you are
My Mother, a Woman, form'd to Obey;
On that Condition all Sexes Priviledges
Are founded, Creating Hand has mixt
Softness and kindness in your Composition,
To Charm and bond the Mind of Man Impatient
Of the Ignoble Pleasure; you were made for
The weakness and necessities of Nature.
Ill are your feeble Souls for Greatness suited,
Desire of Government is Monstrous in you.

QUEEN

Thou mighty Goddess Nature! dost thou hear
This Rebel Son! this insolent Upbraider!
Still fondly Nurst in my indulgent Bosom!
To build whose future Greatness to the Skies,
My Anxious Soul has labour'd more than when
I felt a Mothers Sorrow for his Birth,
Ungrateful Boy!—
Know Fool! that vaunt'st thy self upon thy Manhood,
The greatest he thy rougher kind e're had,
Must have conses't Woman's Superiour Wit,
And own'd our Sexes just Prerogative.
Did not a Mother's fondness plead hard for thee,
Thy Head should pay the sorfeit of thy Insolence;
For know (Young King!) that I am Fate in Persia,
And Life and Death depend upon my Pleasure.

ARTABAN

The World would be well govern'd, should the God's
Depute their Providence to Women's Care,
And trust them with the Fate of Kings and Empires.

QUEEN

Yet thou art Safe! away! nor tempt me farther,
The Patience ev'n of God's themselves has limits,
Tho' they with long sorbearance view Man's Folly.
Yet if thou still persist to dare my Power,
Like them I may be urg'd to loose my Vengeance,
And tho' thou wer't my Creature, stike thee dead.

MIRZA

'Befeech you Sir, retire; the Queen your Mother
Labour's with wisest fore sight for yout Good,
And is incens'd to see you thwart that purpose.

ARTABAN

What is the good of Greatness but the Power?
Madam I leave you; my own Innate Virtue
Arms me against your Rage Unjust and Impotent,
Wait but the great Success my Soul divines
And you will own your little jugling Arts
Have only serv'd to obstruct a while my Glory,
And Skreen this elder Brother ftom my Conquest.

[Exit **ARTABAN** and **CLEANTHES**.

QUEEN

Some Envious pow'r above, some Hostile Demon,

Works under-hand against my stronger Genius,
And counter-mines me with Domestick jars.
Malicious Chance! when all abroad was safe,
To start an unseen Danger from my self!
Mirza! did'st thou not mark the haughty Boy?
With what assuming Pride he own'd his daring?
And claim'd superiority of Power?
Oh can I live, and bear to be Controul'd?
To Share the pleasure of Supreme Command,
With him or any one? Oh Artemisa!
Did'st thou disdain subjection to a Husband,
The Proudest Title of that Tyrant Man?
And canst thou yield t' a Boy? A Son? By Nature
And grateful Duty to Obedience bound?

MIRZA
Madam, Let me intreat you, by the God's,
To Calm your just Resentments; Medling Fortune,
(Whose malice labours to perplex the Wise,)
If not prevented, will unravel all
Those finer Arts, which we with Care have wove.
The Prince, led on by this pernicious honour,
May set the Pris'ners free, think, if that happen,
To what a shock of Fate we stand expos'd.

QUEEN
'Tis true! this foolish honour ruine's all,
Ridiculous Notion! as if, self-Interest
Were not the first and noblest Law of Nature.
Say then wise Lord, and let thy ready Wit,
Still present to it self, avert this blow.

MIRZA
One Method tho' ungentle yet remains
To remedy the Fears this ill produces;
This instant let a Guard confine the Prince;
E're he can gain the means t' Effect that Mischief
He meditates against himself, and us:
To Morrow, early as the Morning dawn's
The Prisoners all shall Die; that once dispatcht,
This raging fit of Honour will relax,
And give him leisure to consider coolly,
Th' Advantage of his Fortune.

QUEEN
You have Reason;
And tho' I fear his haughty Temper will
But badly brook Confinement, he must learn

To bear it as he can, perhaps 'twill bend him
And make his Youth more plyant to my Will.

MIRZA
Your Orders cannot be dispatch't too soon,
Each Minute of the flying Hours is Precious.

QUEEN
The Eunuch Bagoas! let him attend us,
He shall receive Instructions on the Instant.

[Exeunt the **QUEEN** and **MIRZA** severally.

SCENE II. Mirza's Palace

Enter **CLEONE** in Man's Habit, with a dark Lanthorn, **BELIZA** following.

CLEONE
Ye gentler Powers who View our Cares with Pity,
Lend your Compassion to the poor Amestris;
Oh my Belisa, was not thy Soul wounded,
To hear, (when now we past by her apartment)
The piercing Accents of her loud Complainings?
By Heaven my aching Heart bleeds for her Sufferings.

BELIZA
'Tis sure she feels the bitterest Pangs of Woe,
And were not all my Thoughts to you devoted,
Her Grief would deeply sink into my Soul;
Why will you tempt alone ten thousand Dangers?
Your Father's and the furious Queen's Resentments?
The Cruel Guards? And all those fatal Accidents,
Which in the horror of this Dreadful Night
Might shock the Resolution of a Man?

CLEONE
Prithee no more; thou know'st I am resolv'd,
And all thy kind Advice is urg'd in vain.
Thy sond mistaking Fears present the Danger
More dreadful than it is; this Master-key
Admits me thro' that Passage to the Temple,
By which the Guards who seiz'd th' unhappy Prince

[Sighs.

This Morning enter'd; that of all the rest

Is only left unguarded, and from thence
Assisted by the friendly Vail of Night,
We may Conduct him thro' my Father's Pallace
In safety to the Street; there undistinguish'd
Amongst the busy discontented Croud,
That swarm in Murmuring heaps he may retire;
Nor shall my Father or the Queen e're know
The Pious fraud my Love was guilty of.

BELIZA
Yet still I fear—

CLEONE
No more! retire and leave me,
My drooping Heart sits lighter than it's wont,
And chearfully presages good Success.

BELIZA
Where shall I wait you?

CLEONE
At my own Apartment.

BELIZA
The Mighty Gods Protect you.

CLEONE
Softly! Retire;

[Exit **BELIZA**.

What Noise was that?—The Creature of my fears.
In vain, fond Maid, would'st thou bely thy Sex,
Thy Coward Soul Confesses thee a Woman;
A foolish, rash, fond Woman. Where am I going?
To save my Godlike Hero. Oh my Heart!
It Pants and Trembles; sure 'tis Joy not Fear;
The Thought has given me Courage; I shall save him,
That Darling of my Eyes. what if I fail?
Then Death is in my reach and ends my Sorrows.

[Shewing a Dagger.

Why do'st thou shake, my Hand? And fear to grasp
This Instrument of Fate? If I Succeed,
Yet Artaxerxes will not Live for me;
And my Dispair will want thy friendly Aid.
Death ev'ry way shuts up my gloomy Prospect.

If then there be that Lethe and Elisium
Which Priests and Poets tell, to that dark Stream
My Soul of Life impatient shall make hast.
One healing draught my Quiet shall Restore,
And Love forgotten ne're disturb me more.

[Exit **CLEONE**.

SCENE III. A Night Scene of the Temple of the Sun

Enter **ARTAXERXES** and **MEMNON**.

ARTAXERES
Still 'tis in Vain! This idle Rage is Vain!
And yet, my swelling Passions will have way;
And rend my labouring Breast till they find vent.
Was it for this, ye Cruel Gods, you made me
Great like your selves, and as a King, to be
Your Sacred Image? Was it but for this?
To be Cut down, and Mangled by vile Hands,
Like the false Object of mistaken Worship!
Why rather was I not a Pesant Slave?
Bred from my Birth a Drudge to your Creation,
And to my destin'd load inur'd betimes?

MEMNON
The Malice of our Fate were not Compleat,
Had we not been by just degrees, to Happiness
Rais'd, only to be plung'd the deeper down
In an Abyss of Woes. Early Success
Met and Attended all my youthful Wars;
And when I rush't amidst the dreadful Battle,
The weaker Genij of our Asian Monarchs,
Shrunk from the Force of a Superior Fate;
O're March't they fell, and by my Sword were swept
Like Common beings from the Glorious Field.
Then was the day of joyous Triumph, then
My Soul was lifted high, e'vn to the Stars.
But now! What am I now? O damn'd reverse of Fortune!
Now when my Age would be Indulg'd in Ease,
And joy in Pleasure of my former Fame,
Now I am Curs't; held at a Villains Mercy,
My Foe's Derision and the Scorn of Cowards.

ARTAXERES
Oh! Torture of my Soul! damn'd racking Thought!

Am not I too reserv'd for servile Vassalage?
To be the Subject of a Boys Command?
A Boy by Nature set beneath my Sway?
And born to be my Slave! shall he Triumph?
And bid me Live or Die? Shall he dispose
His Beardless Visage to a Scornful Smile,
And tell me that his Pleasure is my Fate?
No! my disdainful Soul shall struggle out
And start at once from its dishonour'd Mansion.

MEMNON
Oh! Royal thought! Nor shall they keep Death from us,
Altho' it's common means be not in reach.
Shall my Old Soldiers outside rough and hardy,
Scarr'd o're wirh many an honourable Mark
Be cag'd for Publick Scorn? Shall a Dog tell me
Thus didst thou once, and now thou art my Slave;
My foot shall spurn thee, tread upon thy Neck,
And trample in the dust thy Silver Hairs?
Shall I not rather Choak? Hold in my Breath?
Or smear some Wall or Pillar with my Brains?

ARTAXERES
Rage or some God shall save us from Dishonour.
But oh! my Father! Can we take our flight,
Tho' to the Stars and leave my Love behind?
Where is she now? where is my Queen! my Bride!
My Charmer! my Amestris!

MEMNON
Speak not of her.

ARTAXERES
Not speak.—

MEMNON
Nor think of her if possible.

ARTAXERES
Was she not snatch't, torn from my helpless Arms,
Whilst every God look't on and saw the wrong,
Heard her loud Cries which vainly strove to rouse
Their flow unready Vengeance? Was she not
Forc'd from my panting Bosom (yet I live!)
Ev'n on our Bridal Day? Then, when our Flames
Were kindly joyn'd and made but one desire;
Then, when she sigh'd and gaz'd, and blush'd and sigh'd.
When every touch, when every Joy grew fiercer,

And those that were behind were more than Mortal.
To lose her then! Oh!—
And yet you bid me think of her no more?

MEMNON
I do; for the bare mention turns my Brain,
And ev'n now I border upon Madness;
So dreadful is the very Apprehension
Of what may be.

ARTAXERES
Can we make thought go back?
Will it not turn again? Cleave to our Breasts?
And urge remembrance 'till it sting us home?
Ha! Now the Ghastly Scene is set before me;
And as thou said'st it runs me to distraction.
Behold her Beauties form'd for Kings to serve
Held Vile, and treated like an abject Slave!
Helpless amidst her Cruel Foes she stands,
Insulting Artemisa mocks her Tears,
And bids her call the God's and me in vain.

MEMNON
Would that were all.

ARTAXERES
Ha! whither would'st thou drive me?

MEMNON
Did you like me consider that Dog Mirza
Early to Hell devoted, and the Furies,
Born, Nurst, and bred a Villain, you would fear
The worst Effects his Malice could express
On Virtue which he hates, when in his Power.

ARTAXERES
What is the worst?

MEMNON
What my old faltring Tongue
Trembles to utter; Goatish Lust and Rape.

ARTAXERES
Ha! Rape! if there are God's it is impossible.

MEMNON
Oh! dreadful Image for a Father's thought,
To have his only Child, her Sexes boast,

The joy of sight and comfort of his Age,
Dragg'd by a Villain Slave his ruthless Hand
Wound in her Hair, to some remote dark Cell,
A Scene for Horrour fit, there to be blotted
By his foul Lust, 'till Appetite be gorg'd.
Let me grow Savage first, let this old Hand
That oft has blest her in her Blood be drench't;
Let me behold her dead, dead at my foot
To spare a Father's greater Shame and Sorrow.

ARTAXERES
A Father! what's a Father's plague to mine?
A Husband and a Lover! If it can be,
If there is such a hoarded Curse in store,
Transfix me now ye God's, now let your Thunder
Fall on my Head, and strike me to the Centre.
Least if I should survive my ruin'd Honour
And injur'd Love; I should ev'n Curse your Godheads,
Run Banning and Blaspheming thro' the World,
And with my Execrations fright your Worshipers
From kneeling at your Altars.

[Enter **CLEONE** with a dark Lanthorn and Key.

CLEONE
This way the Ecchoing Accents seem to come,
Sure 'tis the wretched Prince! Oh can you hear him
And yet refuse to lend your Aid ye Gods?

ARTAXERES
This Gloom of horrid Night suits well my Soul,
Love, Sorrow, Conscious worth, and Indignation,
Stir mad Confusion in my lab'ring Breast,
And I am all o're Chaos.

CLEONE
Is this, alas!
The State of Artaxerxes, Persia's Heir?
Not one Poor Lamp to chear the dismal shade
Of this huge Holy Dungeon; Slaves Murderers,
Villains that Crosses wait for are not us'd thus;
I'le shew my self.

[She turns the light and comes towards **ARTAXERES** and **MEMNON**.

MEMNON
Ha! whence this gleam of Lght?

ARTAXERES

Fate is at hand, let's hast to bid it welcome,
It brings an end of wretchedness.

CLEONE

Speak lower.
I am a Friend; long live Prince Artaxerxes.

ARTAXERES

What wretch art thou, that hail'st me with a Curse?
Come from that Cloud that Mufles up thy Face,
And if thou hast a Dagger, shew it boldly.
We wish to die.

CLEONE

Think better of my Errand,
I bring you Blessings, Liberty and Life,
And come the Minister of happier Fate;

[Turns the light on her self.

Now down my Blood! down to my trembling Heart,
[Aside.
Nor sparkle in my Visage to betray me.

ARTAXERES

Ha! as I live a Boy! a blushing Boy!
Thou wer't not form'd sure for a Murderers Office,
Speak then and tell me what and whence thou art.

CLEONE

Oh! seek not to unvail a trivial Secret,
Which known imports you not. I am a Youth
Abandon'd to Misfortunes from my Birth,
And never new one Cause to joy in Life,
But this that puts it in my pow'r to save
A Prince like Artaxerxes. Ask no more,
But follow thro' the mazes that I tread,
Untill you find your safety.

ARTAXERES

Thus forbidding
Thou giv'st me cause t' Enquire; are then the Guards,
That when the day went down, with strictest watch
Observ'd the Temple Gates, remov'd or fled?

CLEONE

They are not; but with Numbers reinforc'd

Keep every Passage; only one Remains
Thro' Mirza's Pallace, open to your flight.

MEMNON
Ha! Mirza! there's Damnation in his Name,
Ruin, Deceit, and Treachery attend it;
Can Life, can Liberty or safety come
From him? or ought that has an Int'rest in him?
Rather, suspect this feigning Boy his Instrument,
To plunge us deeper yet, if possible
In Misery; perhaps some happy accident
As yet to us unknown, preserves us from
The utmost Malice of his hate, while here.
This sets his wicked Wit at work to draw us
Forth from this Holy Place, much better be
The Pris'ners of the God's, than wear his Fetters.

CLEONE
Unfortunate Suspicion! what shall I say
To urge 'em to be safe and yet preserve
My wretched self unknown?

ARTAXERES
Surely that Face,
Was not design'd to hide dissembled Malice,
Say Youth art thou of Mirza's House? (as sure thou must,
If thou pretend'st to lead us that way forth;)
And can'st thou be a Friend of Artaxerxes?
Whom that fell Dog, that Minister of Devils,
With most opprobrious Injuries has loaded.

CLEONE
Tho' I am his, yet sure I never shar'd
His hate; shall I Confess and own my Shame [Aside]
Oh Heavens!—[Aside]

MEMNON
Mark th' unready Traytor stammers;
Half-bred and of the Mungril strain of Mischief,
He has not Art enough to hide the Cheat,
His Deep designing Lord had better plotted.
Away! thinks he so poorly of our Wit,
To gull us with a Novice? If our Fate
Has giv'n us up, and mark'd us for Destruction,
Tell him we are resolv'd to meet it here.

CLEONE
Yet hear me Prince; since you suspect me sent

By Mirza, to ensnare you, know I serve,
Oh God's! to what am I reduc'd!
[Aside]
—His Daughter;
Some God Compassionate of your Woes has stirr'd
A Woman's pity, in her softer Breast:
And 'tis for her I come to give you Liberty.
I beg you to believe me.

[She Weeps.

ARTAXERES
See he Weeps!

MEMNON
The waiting Tears stood ready for Command,
And now they flow to Varnish the false Tale.

ARTAXERES
His Daughter say'st thou? I have seen the Maid,
Dost thou serve her? And could she send thee to me?
'Tis an unlikely Riddle.

MEMNON
Perhaps 'tis meant,
That she who shares his Poysonous Blood, shall share
The Pleasure of his Vengeance, and inure
The Woman's Hands and Eyes to Death and Mischief.
But thou her Instrument, be gone and say,
The Fate of Princes is not sport for Girls.

CLEONE
Some Envious power blasts my Pious purpose,
And nought but Death Remains; O that by that
I might persuade him to believe and trust me;
And fly that Fate which with the Morning waits him.
I grieve my Lord to find your hard Suspicion,
Debars me from preserving your dear Life
(Which not your own Amestris wishes more)
To Morrow's dawn (oh! let me yet prevail!)
The Cruel Queen resolves shall be your last.
Oh fly! Let me Conjure you save your self.
May that most awful God that here is worship'd
Deprive me of his chearful Beams for ever,
Make me the wretched'st thing he sees while living,
And after death the lowest of the Damn'd
If I have any thought but for your safety.

ARTAXERES

No I have found the Malice of my Mistress,
Since I refus'd her Love when she was proffer'd
By her Ambitious Father for my Bride,
And on a worthier Choice bestow'd my Heart,
She vows Revenge on me for slighted Beauty.

CLEONE

My Lord you do her most unmanly wrong,
She own's the Merit of the fair Amestris,
Nor ever durst imagine she deserv'd you.
Oh spare that thought, nor blot her Virgin's Fame.
In silence still she wonder'd at your Vertues
Blest you, nor at her own Ill Fate repin'd;
This wounds her most, that you suspect unkindly
Th' Officious Piety that would have sav'd you.
Careless of an offended Father's Rage;
For you alone concern'd she charg'd me, guide you
When Midnight Sleep had clos'd observing Eyes,
Safe thro' her Father's with this Key—
And if I met with any that durst bar
Your Passage forth she bid me greet him thus—

[Stabs her self

ARTAXERES [Catching her as she falls]
What hast thou done rash Boy?

CLEONE

Giv'n you the last,
And only Proof remain'd that could convince you,
I held your Life much dearer than my own.

MEMNON

Horrid Amazement Chills my freezing Veins!

CLEONE

Let me Conjure you with my latest Breath,
Make hast to seize the means that may preserve you,
This Key amidst the Tumult of this Night

[Giving the Key.

Will open you a way thro' Mirza's Palace,
May every God Assist and Guard your flight;
And oh when all your hopes of Love and Glory
Are Crown'd wtih just Success; will you be good
And think with Pity on the lost Cleone.

ARTAXERES
Ten thousand dismal Fancies crowd my Thoughts!
Oh! is it possible thou can'st be she,
Thou most unhappy fair one?

CLEONE
Spare my Shame,
Nor call the Blood that flows to give me Peace
Back to my dying Cheeks. Can you forget
Who was my Father? and remember only
How much I wish'd I had deserv'd your Friendship?
Nay let my Tongue grow bold and say your Love,
But 'twas not in my Fate.

ARTAXERES
What shall I say,
To witness how my grateful Heart is rouch'd?
But oh why would'st thou give this Fatal instance?
Why hast thou stain'd me with thy Virgin Blood?
I swear sweet Saint for thee I could forgive
The Malice of thy Father, tho' he seeks
My Life and Crown, thy Goodness might attone
Ev'n for a Nation's Sins; look up and live,
And then still be near me as my Heart.

CLEONE
Oh Charming Sounds! that gently lull my Soul
To Everlasting Rest; I swear 'tis more
More Joy to die thus blest than to have liv'd
A Monarch's Bride; may every Blessing wait you
In War and Peace; still may you be the greatest,
The Favourite of the God's, and Joy of Men—
I faint! oh let me lean upon your Arm—

[She dies.

ARTAXERES
Hold up the Light my Father; ha! she Swoons!
The Iron hand of Death is on her Beauties,
And see like Lillies nip't with Frost they Languish.

MEMNON
My tough old Souldier's Heart melts at the sight,
And an unwonted Pity moves my Breast,
Ill fated Maid too good for that damn'd Race,
From which thou drew'st thy Being! Sure the God's
Angry e're while will be at length appeas'd

With this Egregious Victim; Let us tempt 'em
Now while they seem to smile.

ARTAXERES
A beam of Hope,
Strike's thro' my Soul like the first Infant light
That glanc'd upon the Chaos; if we reach
The open City, Fate may be ours again;
But oh whate're Success or Happiness
Attend my Life, still fair unhappy Maid
Still shall thy Memory be my Grief and Honour.
On one fixt day in each returning Year
Cypress and Mirtle for thy sake I'le wear,
Ev'n my Amestris thy hard Fate shall Mourn,
And with fresh Roses Crown thy Virgin urn.
'Till in Elisium blest thy gentle Shade
Shall own my Vows of Sorrow justly paid.

[Exeunt.

ACT V

SCENE I. Mirza's Palace

Enter **MIRZA**, **MAGAS**, and **ATTENDANTS** with lights.

MIRZA
Pho! You or'e rate the Danger.

MAGAS
If I do
We err in the Extreams, since you Esteem it
As much too lightly; think you then 'tis nothing
This horrid jar of Tumult and Confusion?
Heads white with Years, and vers'd in long Experience,
Who yet remember all the different Changes
A Rolling Age produces, cannot call
To mind one instance dreadful as this Night.
Infernal Discord hideous to behold,
Hangs like it's evil Genius o're the City,
And lend's a Snake to every vulgar Breast.
From several Quarters the mad Rabble swarm
Arm'd with the Instruments of hasty Rage,
And in Confus'd disorderly Array
Most formidable March; their differing Clamour's,
Together join'd Compose one deasning sound;

Arm! Arm! they Cry, Religion is no more,
Our God's are slighted, whom if we revenge not
War Pestilence and Famine will ensue,
And Universal ruin swallows all.

MIRZA

A Crew of mean unthinking heartless Slaves,
With ease stirr'd up to Mutiny and quell'd
With the same ease, with like Expressions shew
Their Joy or Anger both are noise and tumult.
And still when Holidays make Labour cease,
They meet and Shout; do these deserve our Fears?

MAGAS

Most certainly they may; if we consider
Each Circumstance of Peril that Concurrs;
Tigranes with the rest that scap'd the Temple,
Are mixt amongst this Herd, and urge the Wrongs
Which with the God's their Prince and Memnon suffer.

MIRZA

Nor need we fear ev'n that, safe in the Aid
And Number of our Friends, who treble theirs,
For this mad Rout that hum and swarm together
For want of somewhat to Employ their Folly;
Indulge 'em in their fancy for Religion.
Thou and thy Holy Brotherhood of Priests,
Shall in Procession bear the sacred Fire,
And all our Golden God's; Let their Friends Judge
If still they look not kindly as of Old;
'Tis a most apt Amusement for a Crowd,
They'll gaze, and gather round the gaudy Shew,
And quite forget the thoughts of Mutiny;
A Guard shall wait you.

MAGAS

Why go not you too with us?
They hold your Wisdom in most high regard,
And will be greatly sway'd by your persuasion,
Th' occasion is well worth your Care and Presence.

MIRZA

O! you'll not need my Aid: Besides, my Friend,
My Hours this Night are destin'd to a Task
Of more import, than are the Fates of Millions
Such groveling Souls as theirs. As yet the secret
Is Immature nor worth your present knowledge;
To Morrow that and all my Breast is yours.

I must not, dare not trust him with my weakness,
'Twill mark me for his scorn, 'tis yet some Wisdom
If we must needs be fools to hide our folly.

MAGAS
He means the Pris'ners death, let him engross
The Peoples hate, Monopolize Damnation,
I will be safely Ignorant of Mischief
Hereafter when your Wisdom shall think fit
To share those thoughts, and trust 'em with your Friend,
I shall be pleas'd to know; This instant Hour,
My Cares are all employ'd on my own Province,
Which hast's me hence.

MIRZA
May all your God's assist you.

[Exeunt.

SCENE II. An Apartment in Mirza's Palace

Enter **AMESTRIS**.

AMESTRIS
Will ye not hear ye ever Gracious God's?
Since sure you do not Joy in our Misfortunes,
But only try the strength of our frail Vertue.
Are not my Sorrows full? Can ought be added?
My Royal Lord! and Father! ye dear Names
In which my All of Happiness was summ'd.
What have the Ministers of Fate done with you?
Are you not dead? too sure! that's past a doubt;
O Memnon! oh my Prince! my Father! oh my Husband!

[Enter **MIRZA**.

MIRZA
Such Juno was (except alone those Tears)
When, upon Ida's top, she Charm'd the God
That long had been a Stranger to her Bed;
Made him forget the Business of the World,
And lay aside his Providence, t' Employ
The whole Divinity upon her Beauty.
And sure 'twas worth the while, had I been Jove,
So had I too been pleas'd, to be deceiv'd
Into Immortal Joys. Oh cease thy Tears!—

AMESTRIS

Give 'em me back, or if the Grave and Thou
Restore to none, oh joyn my Fate to theirs;
Shut us together in some silent Vault,
Where I may sit and Weep 'till Death's kind Hand
Shall lay me gently by my Lord's dear side,
And hush my Sorrows in Eternal Slumber.

MIRZA

In pity to your form asswage those Tears,
Sorrow is Beauty's bane; nor let your Breast
Harbour a Fear; I wage not War with fair ones;
But wish you would efface those ugly thoughts,
That live in your remembrance to perplex you;
Let Joy, the Native of your Soul return,
And love's gay God sit smiling in your Eyes,
As E'rst he did; I wish you wondrous well,
And would so fully Recompence the Loss
You fondly Mourn, that when you count the Gains,
Your self should own your Fortunes are well chang'd,

AMESTRIS

Oh Impious Comforter! talk'st thou of Joy,
When Nature dictates only Death and Horrour?
Is there a God can break the Laws of Fate?
And give me back the pretious lives I've lost?
What nam'st thou Recompence? Can ought attone
For Blood? a Father's and a Husband's Blood?
Such Comfort brings the Hungry Midnight Wolf,
When having slain the Shepheard, smear'd with Gore,
He leaps amid'st the helpless bleating Flock.

MIRZA

Away with this Perversness of thy Sex,
These foolish Tears, these peevish Sighs and Sobbings!
Look up be gay and Chear me with thy Beauties,
And, to thy wish I will Indulge thy Fancy,
Not all the imagin'd Splendor of the God's
Shall match thy Pomp, sublimely shalt thou Shine
The Boast and Glory of our Asian World;
Nor shall one She of all thy towring Sex
Outrival thee (thou lovely fair) in Power,
Oh think on Power, on power and place Supreme.

AMESTRIS

There is but one, one only thing to think on,
My Murther'd Lord and his dark gaping Grave,

That waits unclos'd impatient of my coming.

MIRZA
Oh listen gentle Maid while I impart
A Story of such softness to thy Ear,
As (like the Halcyon brooding o're the Waves)
May with its influence hush thy stormy Griefs.

AMESTRIS
Begone, and if thou bear'st one thought of Pity
In that hard Breast; oh leave me to my self,
Nor by thy presence hideous to my Soul,
And horrid Consolations strive to add
To my full woes that swell'd without thy help,
All ready rise and bubble o're the Margent.

MIRZA
What if I talk'd of Love?

AMESTRIS
Of Love! oh Monster!

MIRZA
If Love be Monstrous so is this fair Frame,
This Beauteous World, this Canopy the Sky;
That sparkling shines with Gems of Light innumerable,
And so art thou and I; since Love made all;
Who kindly reconcil'd the jarring Atoms
In friendly league, and bid 'em be a World.
Prime not thy lovely Mouth then to Blaspheme
Thy great Creator, thou art his, and made for
His more peculiar Service; thy bright Eyes,
Thy moist Red Lip, thy rising snowy Bosom,
Thy every part was made to furnish Joy,
Ev'n to a riotous Excess of Happiness;
Oh give me but to tast thy blissful Charms,
And take my Wealth, my Honour, Power, take all,
All, All for Recompence.

AMESTRIS
Execrable Wretch!
Thus! Is it thus thou would'st asswage my Sorrows?
When thy inhuman Bloody Cruelty,
Now with redoubling Pangs cleaves my poor Heart,
Com'st thou bespotted with the recent Slaughter
To proper Impious Love? accursed Fiend!
Horror and Grief shall turn me to a Fury,
Still with my Ecchoing Cries, I will pursue thee,

And hallow Vengeance in thy guilty Ears;
Vengeance for Murther! for my Prince's Murther!
And so, my poor old Father think not Villain
Who art the plague and scourge of Human kind;
That there is Peace for thee whilst I run Mad
With raging Sorrow; Vengeance, Vengeance waits thee
Great as my Woes!—My dear! dear! Artaxerxes!

MIRZA

I am not lucky at the glossing Art
Of catching Girls with words, but 'tis no matter,
Force is a sure resort, and when at last
Fierce as a towring Falcon from her height,
I stoop to strike the Prey, it is my own.
Obstinate Fool! how dar'st thou Cross my wishes:
Since the same hand that has aveng'd me well,
Upon my other Foes Commands thy Fate,
Tho' Mercy in Compassion of thy Beauty
Reach out her Hand to save thee, yet if urg'd
Revenge may still take place; think well on that.

AMESTRIS

That, that is all the Mercy which I ask,
Indulge thy thirsty Malice in my Blood,
And hasten me to Peace. My Woman's Heart
Shall gather all it's little stock of Courage
To Arm me for the blow. Tho' Death be terrible,
Ghastly and Pale; yet I will joy to meet him;
My better Life already is destroy'd,
Imperfect now and wanting half my self,
I wonder here in vain, and want thy Hand
To guide and re unite me to my Lord.

MIRZA

Alas! thou hast not read aright thy Destiny,
Matter of much import requires thy Life,
And still detains thee here; Come, I'll instruct thee,
And put thee in the way of Fates Design.

[Laying hold on her.

AMESTRIS

Unhand me Villain!

MIRZA

Nay you must not struggle,
Nor frown and look askew; fantastick Sex!
That put Men on the drudgery to force you

To your own Satisfaction.

AMESTRIS
Let me go,
Abhorr'd detested Monster! Shall he brave you
You awful God's? Shall not your lightning blast him?

MIRZA
Oh no! Your God's have pleasures of their own,
Some Mortal Beauty Charms the wanton Jove,
Within whose Arms he Revels; nor has leisure
To mind thy foolish screaming.

AMESTRIS
Hear me now, sweet Heaven,
Save me ye God's! oh save me! save me! save me!

MIRZA
Come! come along! you see you strive in vain.

[Striving with her.

AMESTRIS
Is there no hope of Aid from God's or Men?
Oh let me turn to thee then, kneel to thee,
And with my Pray'rs and Tears implore thy Pity.

MIRZA
Speak, for Inchantment dwells upon thy Tongue,
And all the flattering Spirits in my Blood
Dance nimbly on to the Coelestial Sound.

AMESTRIS
What shall I say to move him to Compassion?
Thus groveling, prostrate thus upon the Earth,
Let me Conjure you, spare my Virgin Honour,
Spare to commit a Wrong to you unprofitable;
Yet worse to me than Torments, Racks, and Death,
Kill me the last of my unhappy Race,
And let old Memnon's Name with me be lost,
If Death be not enough let me live wretched,
Pull off these Robes and Cloath me like a Slave,
Then send me out to Labour at some Village,
Where I may groan beneath a Cruel Master,
Be hardly us'd and want ev'n Food and Raiment;
'Till Cold, and Dirt, and Poverty shall Change
And make me loathsome as my fellow wretches.
Oh! Let my Rags Claim only this one Priviledge,

To wrap me in the Grave a spotless Maid.

MIRZA
That Tongue which pleads makes all intreating vain,
Thy every Motion, each complaining Accent
Warms me afresh and urges new desire;
Thou art, thou must be mine, not Heaven nor Earth,
Nor the Conspiring power of Hell shall save thee;
I long to lose my Age in thy Embraces,
To bask and wanton in thy warmer Sun
'Till a new Youth shoot thro' me.

AMESTRIS
Chast Diana,
And thou the Guardian of the Marriage-Bed,

[Getting loose from him

Thou Royal Juno! oh protect thy Votary.

MIRZA
My jaded Age and weak Enervate Limbs
Falter and shrink unequal to their Office,
I prithee yield! Come! yield and be a Queen!

[Laying hold on her again

Yield and be any thing! I cannot bear
These fierce convulsive Starts, this raging Flame
That drinks my Blood;

AMESTRIS
Oh! never! never! never!
A Cause like this will turn me to a fighter,
To my last gasp to death I will resist.

MIRZA
My Coward strength! dost thou go back from Beauty?
Rouze and deserve the Pleasure thou would'st tast.

AMESTRIS
Unmanly Traytor!—seize him all ye Fiends.

[In the struggle she draws his own Ponyard and stabs him. **MIRZA** falling.

Damnation! oh my Heart! the cursed Steel
Has struck me to the Earth.

AMESTRIS

There sink for Ever!
Nor rise again to plague the wretched World.

MIRZA

My heated Blood ebbs out, and now too late
My cooler Reason bids me Curse my folly;
Oh! Ideot! Ideot! to be caught so poorly!
Where are thy fine Arts now? Unravell'd all,
Mangled and torn to pieces by a Girl!
Oh Shame of Wisdom! when Revenge was sure,
And Fate was in my grasp, to lose it all,
Neglect the Noble Game, and run out my Years,
On the pursuit of Joys I could not tast;
My Memory must be the jest of Boys.

AMESTRIS

My boasted Courage sinks at sight of Blood,

[Letting fall the Ponyard. **MIRZA** attempting to rise falls again.

Tho' justly shed, and I grow stiff with Horror.
It wo'not be! life gushes out amain,
And I shall die without Revenge or Aid;
What Noise is that? without there! Help!

[Trampling without.

AMESTRIS

Oh Heavens!
What will become of me?

[Enter **ORCHANES** hastily.

ORCHANES

My Lord! where are you?
Bleeding! and on the ground! what wretched Accident?—
Then Fate resolves to make this Night Compleat,
Such as succeeding Horrors ne're shall match.

MIRZA

Oh my Orchanes! I am fall'n vilely,
And this last part of Life will sully all
The Wisdom and Renown of what is past,
Methought thou talk'st of Horrors, speak 'em boldly,
And try if ought can add to this Confusion.

ORCHANES

Prepare, my Lord, and Summon all your Wisdom,
Your utmost Constancy of Soul to hear—

MIRZA
No more! I cannot wait thy Preparation,
Let the ill Fortune take me as it finds me.

ORCHANES
Then hear it thus; your Daughter's dead.—

MIRZA
My Daughter!
Thy words have met with at unguarded side,
And pierce ev'n thro' my Soul. Say, how? where? tell me!—

ORCHANES
As with a Guard I kept the Temple Gates,
I heard old Memnon and the Pris'ner Prince
Loud as the roaring Ocean in a Storm,
Ecchoing their Rage thro' the vast sounding dome,
When on a sudden e're the Night had gain'd
Four hours at most, the Noise was hush'd in Silence,
Wondring and Curious of the Cause, I enter'd,
And found, oh Grief to sight! your lovely Daughter
Drest like a Boy, then warm and newly dead,
One Wound was on her Breast. Why she was there,
Or how we know not; to Compleat the Ill,
The Pris'ners both are fled.

MIRZA
Fled! 'tis impossible!
Ha! which way? whither? how? they could not fly!

AMESTRIS
Oh wond'rous turn of Joy, Are they not dead then?

ORCHANES
They could not scape the Guards, no other Passage
Remain'd but your's, and ev'n that was fast.
Upon the instant I beset each Avenue
Which to your Palace leads; happily as yet
They are not past from thence!

AMESTRIS
Guard 'em ye God's!

MIRZA
Find 'em again Orchanes, e're I die,

Or I am more than double damn'd; this Loss
Is worse than mine, worse than my Daughter's Death,
'Tis Death of my Revenge. Malicious Fortune!
She took the Moment when my Wisdom nodded,
And ruin'd me at once. O doating Fool!
Thou Fool of Love and of pernicious Woman!
I sicken! Nature fails me! oh Revenge!
Will not thy Cordial keep back flying Life?
It shall! Orchanes drag that traitress to me.

AMESTRIS
Oh if thou art a Man I charge thee loose me,
And scorn his bidding, scorn to be his Slave,
A Devil's drudge in Mischief. Save me from Death
Have pity on my Youth, oh spare my Youth!
Orchanes pulls Amestris down to Mirza.

MIRZA
Hearken not to her! drag her! pull her down!
Shall Memnon boast of thee while I die Childless,
No to Cleone's Ghost thou art a Victim,
Oh could I but have seen thee with those Eyes
I view thee now, I had been Wise and Safe;
That Face shall make no more Fools in this World,
Down! bear thy fatal Beauties down to Hell,
And try if thou can'st Charm among'st the Dead.
Die Witch! Enchantress die!

[He stabs her.

AMESTRIS
Ah! Mercy Heavens!

MIRZA
I thank thee Hand at least for this last service,
Now fly Orchanes, hast and tell the Queen
My latest Breath stays for her—Something I would

[Exit **ORCHANES**.

Important to her Service—I Breath short,
Life stays in pain, and struggles to be gone,
I strive in vain to hold it—ha! what mean
These fleeting Shades that dance before my sight?
'Tis Death I feel it plain; the dreadful Change
That Nature starts at. Death!—Death!—what is Death?
'Tis a vast disquisition, Priests and Scholars
Enquire whole Ages, and are yet in Doubt.

My Head turns round!—I eannot form one thought
That pleases me about it,—dying—must resolve me.

AMESTRIS
Oh my hard Fortune! must I die? die now?

[**MIRZA** dies.

When Artaxerxes calls and bids me live.
His dear lov'd Image stays my parting Soul,
And makes it linger in its ruin'd House.
Ha! sure he's dead!—'tis so, and now he stands

[Looking on **MIRZA**.

Arraign'd before the dread Impartial Judges,
To answer to a long Account of Crimes;
Had I but strength perhaps my Fate may yet

[Rising.

Find out a way to save me.
My Love and Father make Life worth my Care,
Alas! My Blood flows fast; this way I think

[Goes off faintly

[Enter at the other side **ARTAXERXES** and **MEMNON** with a Sword and Dark Lanthorn.

MEMNON
Ha! here are Lights! hold up thy Weapon Son.

ARTAXERES
And see Blood! and a Body on the floor!
What means this Scene of Death? what Wretch art thon?
Oh all ye juster Powers 'tis Mirza! see!
He seems now dead.

MEMNON
Damnation then is new to him,
And if there be one deeper pit of Sepulchre,
One Plague above the rest in those dark Regions,
He as the most abandon'd Dog may claim it,
And vie for Preference with Devil's themselves.

[Re-enter **AMESTRIS**.

AMESTRIS

The Doors are guarded; Fate has clos'd me round.

ARTAXERES
Ha! Art thou my Amestris?

MEMNON
Oh! my Daughter!

[They run to her.

AMESTRIS
Are ye then come at last to bless my Eyes
That could not close without one parting view.
Oh hold me or I sink!—

MEMNON
Alas! My Child!—

ARTAXERES
My Cruel Fears! why art thou pale and faint?
Ha! whence this Blood? oh killing Spectacle!

AMESTRIS
Forth from my Heart the Crimson River flows,
My lavish Heart that hastily Consumes
Its small remain of Life: Oh lay me gently
On my last Bed the Earth, whose Cold hard Bosom
Must shortly be the place of my long rest.

MEMNON
What have we done? Or oh if we have fin'd,
What has thy Innocence done to merit this?

AMESTRIS
That Villain Mirza—

MEMNON
Ha! Say what of him.

AMESTRIS
Offer'd most brutal Outrage to my Honour.

ARTAXERES
Oh ye Eternal Rulers of the World!
Could you look on unmov'd? But say, instruct me,
That I may bow before the God that sav'd thee.

AMESTRIS

Sure 'twas some Chaster Power that made me bold,
And taught my trembling hand to find the way
With his own Ponyard to the Villains Heart.

MEMNON
Thou art my Daughter still! oh noble Action!
That gives in Death an Interval of Joy.

AMESTRIS
Just in that hour of Fate a Villain enter'd,
By whose Assistance the revengeful Mirza
Forc'd me to share Death with him.

ARTAXERES
'Tis past, 'tis past;

[Lying down.

And all fires those that lighted up my Soul
Glory and bright Ambition languish now,
And leave me dark and gloomy as the Grave.
Oh thou soft dying swcetness!—Shall I Rage
And Curse my self? Curse ev'n the God's?—Oh no;
I am the Slave of Fate, and bow beneath
The load that presses me; am sunk to Earth
And ne're shall rise again; here will I sit
And gaze 'till I am nothing.

AMESTRIS
Alas! My Lord,
Fain would I strive to bid you not be sad,
Fain would I Chear your Grief; but 'tis in vain;
I know by my own Heart it is impossible;
For we have lov'd too well. Oh mournful Nuptials!
Are these the Joys of Brides? Indeed 'tis hard,
'Tis very hard to part; I cannot leave you,
The Agonizing Thought distracts me; hold me,
Oh hold me fast, Death shall not tear me from you.

ARTAXERES
Oh could my Arms fence thee from Destiny,
The God's might launch their Thunder on my Head;
Plague me with Woes treble to what I feel,
With Joy, I would endure it all to save thee;
What shall I say? what shall I do to save thee?
Grief shakes my Frame, it melts my very Temper;
My manly Constancy and Royal Courage
Run gushing thro' my Eyes; Oh my Amestris!

AMESTRIS

And see my Father! his white Beard is wet
With the sad Dew.

MEMNON

I try'd to Man my Heart,
But could not stand the Buffet of this Tempest,
It tears me up.—My Child! ha! art thou dying?

AMESTRIS

Indeed I am very Sick! oh hold me up,
My Pain encreases, and a Cold damp Dew
Hangs on my Face. Is there no help? no ease?
Have I your Arm my Love?

ARTAXERES

Thou hast; My Heart
Dost thou yet hold.

AMESTRIS

Say will you not forget me?
When I am laid to moulder in my Tomb?
'Tis sure you will not, still there will be room
For my remembrance in your Noble Heart;
I know you lov'd me truly: Now! I faint!
Oh shield me; shield me from that ugly Fantome
The Cave of Death! how dark and deep it is!
I tremble at the sight:—'tis hideous horror!—
The gloom grows o're me—Let me not lie there

[**AMESTRIS** dies.

ARTAXERES

There Life gave way, and the last Rosie Breath
Went in that Sigh. Death like a Brutal Victor
Already enter'd with rudehast defaces,
The lovely Frame he has master'd; see how soon
These Starry Eyes have lost their Light and Lustre!
Stay let me close their Lids. Now for the rest
Old Memnon! ha! Grief has transfix'd his Brain,
And he perceives me not!—Now what of thee?
Think'st thou to live thou Wretch? Think not of any thing,
Thought is Damnation, 'ris the Plague of Divels
To think on what they are! and see this Weapon
Shall Sheild me from it, plunge me in forgetfullness.
Er'e the dire Scorpion thought can rouse to sting me.
Lend me thy Bosom, my cold Bride; Ill Fortune

[Lying by her.

Has done its worst, and we shall part no more;
Wait for me, Gentle Spirit, since the Stars
Together must receive us!

[Stabs himself.

Oh well aim'd!
How foolish is the Coward's fear of Death!
Of Death, the gentlest—surest way to Peace.

[**ARTAXERES** dies.

[**MEMNON** stands looking on the Bodys some time and then speaks.

MEMNON
Yet will I gaze! Yet! Tho' my Eys grow stiff
And turn to Steel or Marble; here's a sight
To Bless a Father! These! These were your Gifts,
Ye bounteous Gods! you'll spare my Thanks for 'em,
You gave me Being too, and spun me out
To hoary Wretchedness; away! 'twas Cruelty!
Oh Cursed! Cursed! Cursed four Score Years!
Ye heap of Ills! Ye Monstrous pile of Plagues!
Sure they Lov'd well, the very streams of Blood
That flow from their pale Bosoms meet and miugle.
Stay, let me view 'em better!—Nay! 'tis thus!—
If thou art like thy Mother?—She dy'd too!—
Where is she?—Ha! that Dog, that Villain Mirza!
He bearsher from me; Shall we not pursue?—
The whirl of Battle comes across me, fly!
Begon! They shall not, dare not brave me thus!
Hey! 'Tis a glorious Sound, rush on my Prince,
We'l start and reach the Goal of Fate at once!

[Runs off

[Enter on the other side **QUEEN** and **ATTENDANTS** with lights.

QUEEN
Why am I Summon'd with this call of Death?
This is no common Ruine; Artaxerxes!
And Memnon's Daughter. Mirza thon art fallen
In pompous slaughter, Could not all thy Arts,
That Dold about destruction to our Enemies,
Guard thy own Life from Fate? Vain boast of Wisdome

That with fantastick Pride, like busie Children,
Builds Paper Towns and Houses, which at once
The Hand of Chance o'erturns and loosly scatters.

1ST ATTENDANT
Oh Dismal Sight,

[Looking out.

QUEEN
What is it frights thy Eys?

1ST ATTENDANT
Old Memnon's Body.

QUEEN
'Tis a grateful Horror.

1ST ATTENDANT
Upon the Floor the batter'd Carcass lies
Weltring in gore, whilst on the Marble wall
A dreadful mass of Brains, Grey Hair, and Blood
Is smear'd in hideous mixture.

QUEEN
Fierce dispair
Has forc'd a way for the impetuous Soul.
'Tis well he is in peace;—What means this Tumult?

[Shout, Clashing of Swords; Enter an **OFFICER**, his Sword drawn.

OFFICER
Fly, Madam, Lest your person be not safe,
The Traytor Bagoas, to whose Charge you trusted
The prince your Son, has drawn the Guards to join him;
And now assisted by the furious Rabble,
On every side they charge those few who keep
This Palace and the Temple, with loud Out-cries,
Proclaiming, that they mean to free the Pris'ners.
Orchanes, e're I fled to give you notice,
Fell by the Prince's hand, the raging Torrent
Bore down our weak resistance, and pursuing
With furious haste, ev'n trod upon my flight.
This instant brings 'em here.

QUEEN
Let 'em come on,
I cannot fear; this Storm is rais'd too late,

I stand secur'd of all I wish already.

[Shout and Clashing of Swords again;

[Enter **ARTABAN**, **CLEANTHES** and **ATTENDANTS**, their Swords drawn.

ARTABAN
Then Virtue is in vain, since base Deceit
And Treachery have triumph'd o'er the Mighty.
Oh! Nature, let me turn my Eyes away,
Lest I am blasted by a Mothers sight.

QUEEN
Ungrateful Rebel! Do thy impious Arms
Pursue me for my too indulgent Fondness
And Care for thee?

ARTABAN
Well has that Care been shewn,
Have you not fouly stain'd my sacred Fame?
Look on that Scene of Blood; the dire Effects
Of cruel Female Arts. But oh! what Recompence;
What can you give me for my murder'd Love?
Has not the Labyrinth of your fatal Counsels
Involv'd my fair, my lovely lost Cleone?
By our bright Gods I swear I will assert
The Majesty of Manly Government,
Nor wear again your Chains, still as our Mother
Be honour'd; rule amongst your Maids and Eunuchs,
Nor mingle in our State, where mad Confusion
Shakes the whole frame, to boast a Womans Cunning.

QUEEN
Thou talk'st as if thy Infant hand could grasp,
Guide and command the Fortune of the World,
But thou art young in pow'r. Remember, Boy,
Thy Father once the Hero of his Age,
Was proud to be the Subject of my Sway,
The Warrior of the Womans Wits gave way,
And found it was his Interest to obey.
And dost thou hope to shake off my Command;
Dost thou? The Creature of my forming hand.
When I assert the Power, thou dar'st invade,
Like Heaven I will resolve to be obey'd,
And rule or ruin that which once I made.

[Exit **QUEEN** and **ATTENDANTS**.

ARTABAN

Let a Guard wait the Queen, tho' nature plead
For reverence to her Person, jealous power
Must watch her subtle and ambitious wit.
Hast thou secur'd the impious Priest Cleanthes?
Magas, that wretch, that prostitutes our Gods.

CLEANTHES

Already he has met the Fate he merited,
This night the Hypocrite in grand Procession
March'd thro' the City to appease the people,
And bore the Gods along to aid his purpose.
When on a sudden, like a Hurricane,
That Starts at once and ruffles all the Ocean,
Some fury more than Mortal seis'd the Crowd;
At once they rush'd, at once they cry'd revenge;
Then snatch'd, and tore the trembling Priest to pieces.
What was most strange, no Injury was offer'd,
To any of the Brotherhood beside,
But all their Rage was ended in his Death.
Like formal Justice that severely Strikes,
And in an Instant is serene and calm.

ARTABAN

Oh! my Cleanthes, do but cast thy Thoughts
Back on the recent Story of this Night;
And thou with me wilt wonder, and confess
The Gods are great and just. Well have you mark't
Celestial powers, your righteous detestation
Of Sacrilege, of base and bloody Treachery.
May this Example guide my future sway;
Let Honour, Truth and Justice crown my Reign,
Ne're let my Kingly word be giv'n in vain,
But ever sacred with my Foes remain.
On these foundations, shall my Empire stand,
The Gods shall vindicate my just Command,
And guard that Power they trusted to my hand.

[Exeunt **OMNES**.

THE EPILOGUE

Spoke by **MRS BRACEGIRDLE**

The Spleen and Vapours, and this doleful Play,
Have mortify'd me to that height to day,

That I am almost in the mortal Mind,
To die indeed, and leave you all behind.
Know then, since I resolve in Peace to part,
I mean to leave to one alone my Heart.
(Last Favours will admit of no Partage,
I bar all sharing; but upon the Stage.)
To one who can with one alone be blest
The peaceful Monarch of a single Breast.
To One—but Oh! how hard 'twill be to find
That Phoenix in your Fickle changing Kind!
New Loves, new Interests, and Religious new,
Still your Fantastick Appetites pursue.
Your sickly Fancies loath what you possess;
And every restless Fool would change his Place;
Some weary of their Peace, and quiet grown,
Want to be hoisted up alost, and shown;
Whilst from the envted height, the wise get safely down.
We find your wavering Temper to our Cost,
Since all our Pains and Care to please is lost.
Must [.....] in vain, supports with Friendly aid
Her Sister Poetry's declining head.
Show but a Mimick Ape, or French Buffoon,
You to the other House in Shoals are gone,
And leave us here to Tune our Crowds alone.
Must Shakespear, Fletcher, and laborious Ben,
Be left for Scaramouch and Harlaquin?
Allow you are unconstant; yet 'tis strange,
For Sense is still the same, and ne're can change;
Yet even in that you vary as the rest;
And every day New Notions are profest;
Nay there's a Wit has found, as I am told,
New ways to Heaven, dispairing of the Old,
He swears he'll spoil the Clerks and Sexion's Trade,
Bells shall no more be rung, nor Graves be made.
The Hearse and Six no longer be in Fashion,
Since all the Faithful may expect Translation.
What think you of the Project? I'm for trying,
I'll lay aside these foolish Thoughts of Dying;
Preserve my Yonth and Vigour for the Stage,
And be translated in a good Old Age.

Nicholas Rowe – A Concise Bibliography

Poems
A Poem upon the Late Glorious Successes of Her Majesty's Arms (1707)
Poems on Several Occasions (1714)

Maecenas. Verses occasion'd by the honours conferr'd on the Right Honourable Earl of Halifax (1714)
Ode for the New Year MDCCXVI (1716)

Original Plays
The Ambitious Stepmother (1700)
Tamerlane (1702)
The Biter (1705)
Ulysses (1705)
The Royal Convert (1707)
The Tragedy of Jane Shore (1714)
Lady Jane Grey (1715)

Adaptations and Translations
The Fair Penitent (1702/3), an adaptation of Massinger and Field's The Fatal Dowry
Lucan (1718), a paraphrase of the Pharsalia
Callipaedia (date unknown), translation of Claude Quillet

Edited Works
The Works of William Shakespear (London: 1709), first modern edition of the plays.

Miscellaneous Works
Memoir of Boileau (date unknown), prefixed to translation of Lutrin
Some Account of the Life of Mr. William Shakespear

www.ingramcontent.com/pod-product-compliance
Lightning Source LLC
Chambersburg PA
CBHW021937040426
42448CB00008B/1117